BOMBER COMMAND
1939–1940

BOMBER COMMAND
1939–1940
The War Before the War

Gordon Thorburn

Pen & Sword
AVIATION

First Published in Great Britain in 2013 by
Pen & Sword Aviation
an imprint of
Pen & Sword Books Ltd
47 Church Street, Barnsley, South Yorkshire S70 2AS

Copyright © Gordon Thorburn, 2013

ISBN 978-1-78159-277-9

A CIP catalogue record for this book is
available from the British Library.

Typeset in 11/13.5pt Palatino by
Concept, Huddersfield

Printed and bound in England by
CPI Group (UK) Ltd, Croydon, CRO 4YY

Pen & Sword Books Ltd incorporates the imprints of Pen & Sword
Archaeology, Atlas, Aviation, Battleground, Discovery, Family History,
History, Maritime, Military, Naval, Politics, Railways, Select, Social History,
Transport, True Crime, and Claymore Press, Frontline Books, Leo Cooper,
Praetorian Press, Remember When, Seaforth Publishing and Wharncliffe.

For a complete list of Pen & Sword titles please contact
PEN & SWORD BOOKS LIMITED
47 Church Street, Barnsley, South Yorkshire, S70 2AS, England
E-mail: enquiries@pen-and-sword.co.uk
Website: www.pen-and-sword.co.uk

Contents

Acknowledgements

Many thanks for help to Dave Fagan, Squadron Leader Dicky James, Jim Shortland, Mitch Williamson.

The Vickers Vimy, first aircraft to cross the Atlantic (in sixteen hours), was a First World War design and standard heavy-bomber equipment for the newly formed Royal Air Force until superceded by its very similar sister, the Vickers Virginia, from 1925 onwards. The Vimy did not entirely disappear from front-line service until 1929.

Spot the difference? The Vickers Virginia served with the RAF until 1936. This is a fairly early version, with squadron members and dog.

CHAPTER 1

But will these bombers get through?

In a statement to the House of Commons on 10 November 1932 on the ever-present topic of world disarmament, Prime Minister Stanley Baldwin said:

> 'I think it well also for the man in the street to realise there is no power on earth that can protect him from bombing, whatever people might tell him. The bomber will always get through.'

Baldwin was not alone in his belief. The common view was that a bombing war would quickly reduce all belligerents to smoking ruins and end civilisation as they knew it. Professor J. B. S. Haldane tried to calm the prophets of doom with his measured forecast that 500 aeroplanes, each carrying two tons of bombs, would kill 20,000 people in one air raid.

It did not seem to matter that there was no evidence anywhere to justify such fears, nor did it matter that no air force had the means to achieve such destruction – yet. The only experience the RAF had had in bombing since the end of the First World War had been in Empire policing. Troublesome folk in the desert could be made less troublesome by the threat or act of dropping bombs from biplanes on undefended villages. It was much more economical than using troops.

On 24 October 1933 Winston Churchill, then a back-bencher in his 'wilderness years', told the House of Commons that Germany was well on the way to becoming the most heavily armed nation in the world, despite the Treaty of Versailles prohibiting rearmament.

1

In March 1934 Prime Minister Baldwin, also addressing the House, promised that if the forthcoming Geneva Disarmament Conference could not reach a satisfactory conclusion, the strength of the RAF would be increased to match the strongest European air force. Said increase duly began in July 1934 with a planned growth to 128 front-line squadrons by 1939. In May 1935 the government decided to add another 1,500 aircraft of all types.

Meanwhile, those frontline squadrons equipped as bombers were saying goodbye to their flights of the Vickers Virginia, a 100mph biplane first flown in 1922 and itself not much more than a modified Vickers Vimy of 1917 vintage; the first aircraft to fly the Atlantic. The Virginia in its final version, the all metal Mark X, was slightly faster – it could overtake a Vimy at about five miles an hour – and could carry more – 3,000lb rather than 2,000lb – and further, 1,000 miles rather than 900, but it still never met the original Air Ministry specification.

That the Virginia was the RAF's main bomber for so long, twelve years and more, was entirely due to government spending priorities. The Air Ministry did issue specification B19 in 1927, looking for a new bomber to replace the Virginia but, with more muddle, and failure to keep up with technical developments, it was apparent that no new bombers would be arriving soon and so fifty more Virginias were ordered.

Although the result of specification B19, the Handley Page Heyford, began coming into service in 1933, the RAF had to hang on to its Virginias and still had a hundred or so of them going into 1936.

Take No. 9 Squadron as an example: they had the Vimy in 1924 and the Virginia from 1925 to 1936. The potential of these aircraft as war machines in Europe is illustrated by an incident in 1927, when a Virginia, flying from Spitalgate, near Grantham, Lincolnshire, to Manston in Kent, got so lost above the clouds that it ended up in The Netherlands.

Meanwhile, No. 9 and other squadrons tested the B19 spec competitors: Fairey Night Bomber, Handley Page Night Bomber, and an enhanced Virginia with different engines. Operations Record Book, Number 9 Squadron:

> 'In the summer (of 1932) pilots of the squadron tested experimental night bombers made by the following firms: Vickers, Handley Page, and Faireys. The census of opinion was in

favour of the Vickers. The H.P. was nice to fly and easy to handle but doubts were expressed concerning the strength of the undercarriage. This collapsed at Upper Heyford for no apparent reason. After repairs the machine was crashed by F/O Matthias of No. 10 Squadron at North Coates Fitties. It caught fire and was burnt out. The Fairey was returned to the makers as the controls were found inadequate. The gliding angle was considered too flat for night flying on small aerodromes.'

This may have been a case of 'better the devil you know' The Fairey was a low-wing monoplane and so of startlingly different appearance to its biplane contemporaries. It eventually appeared as the Hendon; 38 Squadron and 115 Squadron had all fourteen of them from 1937 until January 1939 when it was replaced by the Wellington. The Hendon turned out to be not much of a bomber – in round numbers, 150mph, range 1,400 miles maximum, bomb load only 1,600lb.

The Handley Page may have had a weak undercarriage in proto-type but it became the Heyford and RAF frontline equipment. The Vickers, known as the Type 150 and later the Vanox, was a modified, slightly smaller Virginia. The modifications, of which it had many, were its downfall. ORB, 9 Squadron in May 1933:

'It was found to be too unstable fore and aft to make a good bombing platform, and bombing was particularly difficult in hazy conditions. It offered no greater difficulty than a Virginia for machine gun firing. Successfully flown at night under full war load.'

By now it was the Type 255 and this was the only one ever built. It took part in a simulated raid on the bridge at Stratford-upon-Avon. It didn't hit but gave some useful searchlight practice (on account of its higher ceiling) to the Anti-Aircraft Defence Brigade, though there was no point in keeping on with it when the Heyford and the Hendon were already ordered and in production.

Peacetime training for the bomber squadrons of course included various kinds of exercise. During one in 1934 three Virginias were supposed to attack a fleet of ships off Portland at night. A flying boat signalled to the bombers' base with the fleet's position and they took off. The intention was for the leading bomber to illuminate the ships with parachute flares whereupon the other two would bomb. Alas, there was cloud down to 1,000 feet so they couldn't do it and had to go home.

It would seem, looking across all the different exercises, that good weather was essential for war; so many were cancelled through 'adverse weather conditions'. One of the drawbacks of night flying, it was found, was the need to reset the flare path if the wind changed, and this could take an hour or more. Still, in daylight at the annual Hendon display, the bombers could fly in low to drop bags of flour in an attempt to knock over some giant skittles.

Even when the 'new' Heyford came in, the weather remained supremely important. One flight of seven Heyfords of 102 Squadron, from Northern Ireland to Yorkshire, came across fog and icing at Morecambe which got worse as they flew on. One crew abandoned ship, two more crashed and three made forced landings, one of which was a write-off. There were fatalities too as there frequently were in accidents. Flying was still a dangerous pursuit in itself without the hazards of war. One of the Heyfords was captained by Sergeant Vic Otter:

> 'We maintained an indicated height of 4,000 feet but Sgt Church (second pilot) shouted that we were getting very low. The next I knew I was engulfed in blazing wreckage. There was snow everywhere (on the Pennine moors above Hebden Bridge) and dense, freezing fog. I crawled around seeking my crew but without success.'

Two were already dead and Sergeant Church would die in the ambulance.

The Handley Page Heyford, originating in that 1927 specification, ceased production three years after it came into service in 1933, a remarkably short time-frame for a front-line bomber, which rather indicates just how out-of-date the design was. As it fell out of favour in 1936, the new RAF Commands were formed – Fighter, Bomber, Coastal and Training.

A tea party at RAF Manston in 1928 watches a flypast of Virginias.

The Mark VIII Virginia was modified to provide extra defensive power although, at no more than 100mph with all three gunners in the open, we can hardly imagine much hope of victory. The gunners, in this case (from left) LAC Newton, F/O Harvey and LAC Andrew of No. 9 Squadron, had to clamber out to their turrets after take-off, wearing parachutes, via a ladder and catwalks. Comments coming back from the squadrons resulted in senior officials trying it, and the Mark IX appeared without circus act.

The transition from Virginia to the Heyford was effected without much alarm. It was just another biplane after all, even if one requiring the pilot to take off and land in a cockpit eighteen feet above the ground. Eleven squadrons had 124 Heyfords between them, nos 7, 9, 10, 38, 78, 97, 99, 102, 148, 149 and 166.

Defensive armament comprised three .303 inch machine guns – one in the front turret, one in the dorsal turret, and one in the retractable 'dustbin' underneath. As with the facilities for pilot and observer/second pilot, the two gunners' cockpits were open which, given that the fuselage was fixed to the upper wing, meant that all had a fine field of vision. The other side of that coin was visibility to the enemy. The front gunner especially must have felt vulnerable, standing there, seen from the waist up, swinging his gun around and changing magazines when he ran out of bullets. The man in the dorsal turret could at least drop down into the fuselage when he wanted to get into his dustbin, but once he'd wound that down and out, he was exposed again. One of the gunners operated the wireless when not under fire.

The Heyford's fuselage was metal clad at the front, fabric-covered behind, and all the flying surfaces were fabric on metal frame. It could carry a 3,500lb bomb load but that would have to be much reduced if it was to reach its top speed of 142mph and maximum range of 920 miles. It allegedly had a ceiling of 21,000 feet, although it is not obvious how aircrew al fresco might have managed with no oxygen and in temperatures many degrees below freezing. On one petrol test, a Heyford reached 15,000 feet where the temperature was measured at minus thirteen centigrade.

In the matter of bomb carrying, it marked a kind of interim stage between the exterior racks of earlier craft and the bomb bays of the Second World War machines. The centre section of the lower wing took the bombs, ready fused, in closed cells that were clicked into place by armourers lying on their backs on the ground, and then plugged in to the electrical circuit ready for use. More weaponry could be attached to conventional racks on the lower wing, outboard of wheels that had huge spats, streamlined in a futile attempt to make the damned thing go faster.

Several squadrons took their Heyfords to Mildenhall in October 1937 to show them to a visiting party of German air force staff officers. We can only imagine the Germans' thoughts as they contemplated the RAF's main bomber, knowing that the Messerschmitt 109 was even

The Handley Page Heyford (this is a Mark III) came on strength in 1933 with No. 99 Squadron, ceased production in 1936 but, hardly credibly, was still there in service in March 1939. Top speed 142mph unloaded, range 920 miles with 1,600lb bomb load, much less with the full load of 3,500lb.

'No one can say with absolute certainty that a nation can be knocked out from the air, because no one has yet attempted it.'

Air Chief Marshal Sir Cyril Newall,
Chief of the Air Staff, 1937.

Customs of the Service by A.H.S, published by Gale and Polden at 2s. 6d, points out that it is disastrous to address a Flight Lieutenant as 'Lieutenant', a Group Captain as 'Captain' and a Wing Commander as 'Commander'. Pilot Officers and Flying Officers should be addressed as 'Mr'. Abbreviations in writing should be avoided; few officers, however modest, could survive being described as a P.O. or a W.C. without some sense of disappointment.

then being delivered to the Luftwaffe, an aircraft that would set a new speed record of almost 380mph the following month. All parties also knew what the Luftwaffe, in the guise of the Condor Legion with a mixture of old and new types of aircraft, had done at Guernica and other places in the Spanish Civil War – admittedly largely unopposed but terrifying nonetheless.

The Germans used the Civil War (July 1936–March 1939) to give their airmen experience. There were about 3,000 Luftwaffe air and ground crew in Spain at any one time, but the force was rapidly rotated so that perhaps 30,000 men had training on the job. The conclusions generally were that wholesale bombing of cities did not itself bring victory but the use of bombers, especially dive bombers, as artillery in support of ground forces, was very effective.

The German high command in any case believed that strategic bombing would not be necessary in the forthcoming European war as Britain would not be involved. The defeat of France would come about through defeat of its army, its poorly equipped air force being almost an irrelevance, and so 'co-operation' types of aircraft were the ones on which to concentrate. Although there was a brief surge of emphasis on heavy bombers for the Luftwaffe with various proto-types being designed, its chief proponent, General Wever, was killed in an air crash in 1936 and the enthusiasm died with him.

Also, the high command could not allow limited production capacity to be diverted from their favoured fighters and co-operation fast bombers, to a type for which they could as yet see no use. The mistake was not rectified and Germany never would have a significant force of heavy bombers. Focke Wulf FW200 transport planes would be converted to bombers for the 1940 Norway campaign, and Heinkel He177, with four engines and two propellers, would see service in 1943 against sea-going targets, but that was all.

The fighters had a good time too in the Spanish war, especially the Me109s. One pilot, Lieutenant Balthasar, was reported as shooting down four Martin bombers in one day. He may well have shot down four but they were Tupolev SB, often mis-described as Martins because that's what they should have been, had the Spanish government's order for fifty of same not been refused. The Tupolev was an all-metal, twin-engined light bomber along the lines of the Bristol Blenheim, considered a revolutionary design and very fast in 1934, but was no match for the Me109 as the Luftwaffe generals were delighted to observe.

The giant bombers the Germans never had: top is the Dornier Do19, used in small numbers for training and for experiments in strategic bombing, if not for the real thing. With a crew of ten, including five gunners, carrying a ton and a half of bombs at less than 200mph, it would not have been much good anyway. The project was cancelled after the death of General Wever.

Lower picture is of the Junkers G38, a bomber that never bombed but developed into the Ju90 transport, a luxury version of which became Hitler's personal aircraft.

'No doubt, from a moral point of view, air raids are an unbearable outrage for the civilised man … But if we look coldly at the facts we find that less damage was done than might have been supposed. The number of people killed in Barcelona by bombing in over 250 air raids was no more than 4,357, which is almost identical with the number of deaths caused by street accidents (mainly car accidents) in the city during the same period of time.'

Dr Emilio Mira, *British Medical Journal* June 1939.

'Professor E. Mira of Barcelona University stated that air force men were liable to nervous exhaustion rather than neurosis. The best pre ventive of war-flying neurosis was devotion to the object for which the war was being waged. Group Captain H. L. Burton of the RAF Medical Service said that while anxiety symptoms and sometimes amnesia with hysteria were found amongst airmen, the cause was not actual flying but usually financial and domestic stress. Dr A. McGlashan said that a high degree of suggestibility was induced in the mind of an airman as he sat in the cockpit in darkness and listened with acute attention to the noise of his engine while searchlights combed the sky for him.'

Annual Conference of the Ex-Services Welfare Society, London, July 1939, reported in the *British Medical Journal*.

By September of 1938, with Austria annexed by Germany and obvious threats being made to do the same with the Sudetenland region of Czechoslovakia, the bomber squadrons were put on permanent standby. No. 148 Squadron and six others had the Vickers Wellesley, a single-engined monoplane which was faster and had a longer range than the Heyford, and so these were made ready for a raid on Berlin should the Czech crisis not be resolved. All were loaded with three 500lb bombs carried in torpedo-shaped pods under the wings.

The range and the load meant that the return journey was unlikely to be completed and crews expected to parachute into The Netherlands as they ran out of petrol. Being armed only with one machine gun fixed to fire forward in the starboard wing, and another in the dorsal turret, return would have been made even more doubtful should they have been intercepted.

The first British modern bomber, the Wellington, was still a while away but the Wellesley was an intermediate design on the road to it, with enclosed cockpits and a retractable undercarriage. It was also the first aircraft using Barnes Wallis's geodetic construction. Mathematically, a geodesic line is the shortest possible path between two points in a curved space or, to put it more simply, a geodesic curve is one of which the tangent vectors remain parallel when transported along it.

To put it more simply still, Wallis, inspired by the basket-weave of metal seen in his work on airships, devised a system of criss-crossing curved metal ribs, in effect a lattice or net of duralumin members, which was light yet very strong. He called it geodetic, to distinguish it from geodesic proper, and the engineering principles of stress and torsion at work in it meant that large pieces of the structure could be removed while the load-bearing abilities of the whole remained. As would be shown many, many times in the approaching war, Wellingtons could limp home with seemingly fatal amounts of damage, enough to cause other aircraft to break up in the air.

As it turned out, Czechoslovakia's allies backed away from the threat of war, gave in to the Germans, and Prime Minister Neville Chamberlain came home from Munich famously waving his piece of paper and declaring peace in our time. The bomber squadrons were stood down and debombed, all except one Wellesley of No. 148 that the armourers forgot. This aircraft was flown for another four months before its extra load of 1,500lb was discovered; the pilots meanwhile regarding it as a rogue machine.

In America President Roosevelt leaned the way of Britain and her allies while listening to the war-like rumblings coming from Germany, but involvement of any kind in a future European conflict was by no means a popular notion in the country. Widely read newspaper columnists such as Boake Carter thought the idea ridiculous:

'Where does the Roosevelt Administration derive the idea that Americans want to go gallivanting forth to play Sir Galahad again? The question that Americans should remember is: Do we or do we not want to help one gang of thieves against another gang of thieves? We saved the first crop of thieves twenty years ago – and made the world a safe place for a new set of thieves.'

Walter Winchell, syndicated in 150 newspapers, said:

> 'The future of American youth is on top of American soil, not underneath European dirt.'

A few saw things differently, like Mark Sullivan, but he featured in only forty-six newspapers:

> 'Free government has its principal home in America and Great Britain. If it is destroyed in England by a foreign foe, then it will be more difficult to defend it here. England is our shield.'

Well said, but what sort of a shield was it? The chiefs of the allied armed forces had all been through the Great War that had finished only twenty years before. Nobody could contemplate such a thing happening again; years of struggle between opposing armies going nowhere. This would be a different kind of war, surely, although quite how different nobody knew, except possibly the Germans. One thing all could be certain about. Air power was bound to be a major factor.

It was the view of Winston Churchill – a troublemaker if ever there was one and soon to be Prime Minister – that he who held the skies held the ways and means of military success. Current PM Neville Chamberlain didn't seem to have a view. So what were the chances of Britain holding the skies and thence taking the war to the enemy? We had two superb fighters in the Hurricane and the Spitfire, but they were for defence. What about attack? What about the bombers?

It was obvious to bomber strategists that their job would be a hard one. All thought was of precision targets; that meant going in daylight because such targets could not be found at night. If they were to go in daylight, the only way they could reach their targets would be if they could defend themselves against fighter attack and somehow avoid the shooting from the ground.

Flying in close formation with cloud cover could be the answer if it were possible to keep formation in the clouds when bomber crews couldn't see each other. Keeping formation while attacking and while under attack would also be difficult, which made things doubly questionable when the tight formation was the given means of defence.

In an article titled 'A New European Aircraft Carrier?' in the May 1939 issue of *L'Ala d'Italia* Mario Muratore discussed the possibilities of aerial attack on Germany using aircraft bases in Poland.

French and British squadrons taking off from Metz would be able to land in Poland after a flight of 800 kilometres which would carry them over important German industrial and military objectives, and after reforming at Polish bases they could return to France and repeat their bombing operations on the way home.

'Present heavily loaded bombers of the multi-engined type are, and will be, at least 80mph slower than interceptor fighters, and I consider it very doubtful whether a sufficient number of machines would reach their target, except under special conditions such as in poor weather and at night.'

H. P. Folland, designer of the De Havilland SE5 and Gloster Gladiator, June 1939.

'No country has yet had extensive experience in modern aerial warfare, and although certain experience has been gained in the Spanish Civil War and in China, these can only be compared to an Air Force Pageant in relation to what aerial warfare between two powerful nations would be.'

H. P. Folland, June 1939.

Flying too quickly for the ground gunners would also be good if only there were an aircraft that could go that fast. Having long-range fighter escorts would also be very welcome, if only such were available.

Here was a most ingenious paradox: the bombers would always get through, if there were any bombers that could do it. The RAF certainly didn't have any. Added to that, they had no real idea about the defensive strengths and abilities of their likely opponents in Germany in the air or on the ground.

Of course, the Germans didn't have any bombers either, at least, not ones suitable for strategic bombing of Britain from aerodromes in the fatherland. Hitler saw the Luftwaffe as a dramatically effective addition to the army, the Wehrmacht, not as an offensive force on its own. Besides, he had no intention of going to war with Britain, at least until 1942.

In America, the prototype 300mph Boeing B17, the four-engined Flying Fortress, had flown in 1935 and was about to come into service with the USAAF. The first British four-engined bomber, the inadequate Short Stirling, was being developed but would not fly in anger until February 1941. The Handley Page Halifax came shortly after, while the Avro Lancaster hadn't been thought of yet.

According to Air Ministry figures, the airspeed of bombers progressed thus in ten years (given in mph):

	1929	1934	1939
Light	Fox 160	Hart 184	Battle 257
Medium	Sidestrand 144	Overstrand 152	Blenheim 295
Heavy	Virginia 104	Heyford 142	Hampden 265
		Hendon 156	Wellington 265

The definition of a heavy bomber was really little more than the heartiest twin-engined beast we have at the moment, and obviously does not compare with the later four-engined heavies. None of the 1934 bombers could have reached a target in Germany with a worthwhile bomb load and got home again. Why the Blenheim was classified as medium is not clear.

Regarded as modern enough for war in 1939 was the Armstrong Whitworth Whitley, aka the 'flying barn door'. It was a twin-engined monoplane with a retractable undercarriage and enclosed movable gun turrets front and rear, but with only one gun in each (although in the Mark III that was increased to two at the back), a power-operated turret at the front, plus a retractable dustbin turret with two guns that slowed down an already slow aircraft. The Mark V would have Rolls Royce Merlins but even with them it could only do 230mph, and much less with a full load of 7,000lb of bombs. It was classified as a night bomber and so its lack of speed and agility were not considered so important at the time, and it compared very favourably with the biplane 'heavy' bombers it was replacing.

As was common practice, the original design had bomb-bay doors that opened when the bombs hit them, which did not help bombing accuracy, but later models had hydraulic doors. The Mark V also had a four-gun, hydraulic rear turret, so didn't need the dustbin. Marks II, III, IV and V were all on the strength when the war began but not so many of the V. They all had a crew of five: pilot, second pilot/observer, bomb-aimer/gunner, wireless operator, rear gunner.

The Handley Page Hampden – the 'flying suitcase' – a daylight medium bomber with two engines, entered service in late 1938. It was fast for its time – 265mph maximum – could carry 4,000lb of bombs and was much more manoeuvrable than the Whitley. Its defences were its weakness; one fixed and one movable gun up front, and one (later twins) under the tail boom and on its back. The crew of four – pilot, second pilot who was also observer/bomb aimer/front gunner, wireless operator/gunner, rear gunner – complained about being packed in like sardines, but the aircraft was more generally known as the 'suitcase' rather than the 'sardine tin', also the 'flying tadpole' because of its looks.

Crew members could not see each other and the boys in the back had little benefit from the underpowered heating system. Without the classic attributes of the rock climber – flexibility and superb power-to-weight ratio – it was as good as impossible in flight for the second pilot to take over should the captain be incapacitated.

It was nevertheless a popular machine with pilots who found it easy to fly, manoeuvrable, with good visibility and sensitive controls. Its major foible, which those pilots soon found out about and learned how to avoid, was its liability to translate a sharp turn to port, or a failure of the port engine, into a sideslip and then a flip onto its back, resulting in a fatal spin.

Flying Officer Guy Gibson, later Wing Commander VC, DSO, DFC and Dambusters hero, a Hampden pilot with 83 Squadron, didn't mention that particular fault:

'C Charlie was my own aeroplane and a lousy one at that. On take-off she swung like hell to the right and flew with her left wing low. Sometimes an engine died out, but that was nothing. We loved her because she was ours.'

The Hampden was really obsolete before it went into action and should never have been used on the long-range raids when the bombing war began in earnest after the fall of France. If it was carrying a 2,000lb bomb load it could stay in the air for ten hours. The trip to Berlin and back for an aircraft of the Hampden's speed was nine hours minimum, assuming good weather and favourable winds, and many a Hampden would be lost at sea as its petrol ran out coming home.

Also fast were the Bristol Blenheim – the Mark I was faster than most of the fighters flying in 1936 – and the single-engined Fairey Battle, an elegant machine looking rather like a stretched-out Spitfire or Hurricane. These two were both light bombers, carrying a maximum of 1,000lb armament, although the Battle could carry another 500lb on wing racks. The Battle was poorly armed, with one gun fixed in the wing to fire forward and one at the back of the cockpit, and underpowered with one engine to propel an aircraft almost as big as the Blenheim, although that engine was the Rolls Royce Merlin in its first RAF application.

It had been designed to an Air Ministry specification of 1933, the round numbers of which suggest that perhaps the matter had not been considered too deeply. It wanted a two-seater, single-engined monoplane day-bomber to carry 1,000lb of bombs for 1,000 miles at 200mph.

By 1937, when the production model flew, that lack of forethought was clear to those in authority who decided that light bombers were not going to be much good for attacking burgeoning enemy Germany. Still, they had to keep pace with the Luftwaffe somehow so they kept on building, and squadrons nos 52, 63, 88, 105 and 226 all had Battles by the end of that year.

The Bristol Blenheim had curious origins, deriving from a fast passenger aircraft first ordered by Lord Rothermere as his private transport. The military version was, like the Battle, poorly armed with a fixed gun in the port wing and another in a dorsal turret. Speed would be its defence, which was a sound enough policy at the time. It had a crew of three – pilot, observer/bomb aimer, wireless-operator/gunner. When the war began the Blenheim was in its Mark IV version with more powerful engines, twin guns in the turret and a longer range, making it more suitable for reconnaissance although it was still seen as a bomber, a role for which it was not so suitable.

Best of all by far was the Vickers Wellington, designed by Barnes Wallis. It doubled the Heyford biplane's performance, taking 4,500lb of bombs 1,500 miles at 240mph, and it could reach up to 18,000 feet although its ceiling in practical terms was rather lower. It was equivalent as a bomb-carrier to the B17 Fortress but, with much less defensive armament, two engines fewer and its fuselage made of metal net covered in fabric, it was a great deal cheaper to build.

Exercises were stepped up – for many still in Heyfords and Wellesleys – after the Munich Agreement. In December No. 9 Squadron fielded eight Heyfords 'with full crews to take part in the No. 3 (Bomber) Group Monthly Tactical Exercise. Owing to inclement weather however, no raids were attempted.' The squadron CO, Wing Commander Smith MC, had recently been killed when his Heyford hit a tree at night and burned out, but the squadron was brought back to full establishment of sixteen aircraft, twelve to be kept in readiness and four in reserve. Meanwhile, in October 1938 No. 99 Squadron took delivery of its first Wellingtons to replace their Heyfords, and a few weeks later 38 Squadron also had Wellingtons delivered to replace their Fairey Hendons. Reformed from a flight of 99 Squadron, No. 149 changed over from Heyfords to Wellingtons in the New Year of 1939, as did No. 9 Squadron, four months later than expected. While they waited, pilots had been instructed by 148 Squadron members in Wellesleys, in the matter of flaps, retractable under-carriages and the Bristol Pegasus engine.

The Handley Page Harrow was another 1930s bomber design found to be unsuitable once it went into service. It first flew in 1936 as Handley Page got busy with an order for 100, and entered service with 214 Squadron in 1937. It was redesignated as a transport plane by the time war broke out.

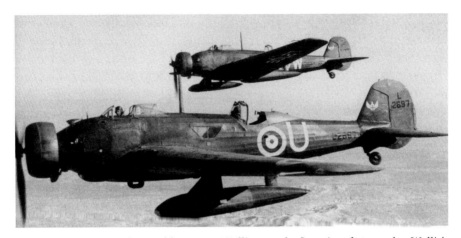

The Vickers Wellesley, designed by Barnes Wallis, was the first aircraft to employ Wallis's radical 'geodetic' construction, a rigid network of slim metal members. Seven squadrons of Wellesleys were on standby to attack Germany should the Munich peace talks of 1938 fail, but they were replaced by the much better Wellington by the time the war began.

'Today the aeroplanes supplied in quantity to the Royal Air Force are technically as good as, or better than, those in other air forces.'

F. Handley Page, President of the Society of British Aircraft Constructors, July 1939.

'The German Air Force is replacing older types with the following new ones: Messerschmitt Bf 110, a twin-engined fighter, Junkers Ju 88, a twin-engined bomber, and finally the Dornier 215, also a twin-engined bomber.'

French magazine *L'Air*, June 1939.

'Hans Dieterle, the German pilot who broke the international speed record last March, when he achieved a speed of 462 miles an hour with a Messerschmitt, has expressed the opinion that speeds of over 600 mph will become practical within the next three years.'

Italian magazine *L'Aquilone*, June 1939.

In March No. 148 swapped their Wellesleys for Wellingtons, followed by No. 115. Reformed from a flight of 38 Squadron, No. 115 had Hendons to start with, which were replaced by the Handley Page Harrow – also found to be unsuitable as a bomber and so redesignated as a transport craft.

In May 1939 No. 9 Squadron was informed that it was to provide the main British entertainment at the Military Aviation Meeting in Brussels at the Évere aerodrome. Operations Record Book:

> 'Ten machines were to go; nine for the display and one as a spare. Training was commenced immediately by the Squadron, and flying crews were provisionally chosen so that the personnel would have the maximum opportunity of getting used to one another.'

Having become so used, they would fly past in several formations – vic (that is, in a V), line astern, echelon to starboard and, seeking to impress as was clearly the purpose, they would make figure-of-eight runs while thus arranged. It was hardly Red Arrows stuff but it would be nerve-racking enough, knowing that the world was watching.

The display date was Sunday 9 July. After many difficulties in finding sufficient spares for ten operational Wellingtons, and a delay in departure due to bad weather, the squadron loaded up (40lb luggage allocation for officers, 30lb for airmen) and arrived at Évere on the evening of 8 July, to find that the doors of the hangars were not wide enough to take a Wellington straight in. During a sweaty battle of an hour and a half, the aircraft were pushed and pulled and swung back and forth until they were safely housed, and the officers could repair to their hotels:

> '... for our first glass of continental biere. Our thirst quenched, we went to our rooms where we were, it is to be confessed, a little staggered by the luxury, and a trifle surprised by the absence of valets de chambre and the presence of femmes de chambre. Resolving firmly not to be surprised at anything, we changed into Mess kit for the Banquet in the Salle des Glaces, Palais d'Egmont.'

Sumptuous and tediously long though the banquet was, the spirits of the RAF representatives were not cast down and 'the whole squadron sallied forth with the Belgian officers to taste the night life of Brussels'.

Next day there was a truly magnificent display of flying, although the Germans and the French were not showing their hands in their latest types of aircraft. The French did complex aerobatics in Morane Parasols (First World War machines now used for training) and the Germans similarly flew their advanced trainer, the very agile Bücker-Jungmeister, a single-engined biplane that would go on to dazzle air-show crowds for many years. The Belgians flew Gloster Gladiator biplane fighters, and one RAF Hurricane put on a high speed array of aerial tricks and turns to complement Europe's first look at a modern RAF bomber squadron. There was a crash. A German pilot overdid it in his Jungmeister and was killed.

Another formal dinner that evening was followed by a tourist day in Liège and a Guest Night at a château organised by the Belgian officers:

> 'Here a most enjoyable and rather hilarious evening was spent, greatly aided by the presence of a great deal of beauty in the form of the girlfriends of Belgian officers. It has been rumoured that English officers, unable to speak a word of French at 20.00 hours were, by the small hours, conversing fluently in that language.'

The august editor of *Aeronautics* magazine, Oliver Stuart, was at the same show:

> 'The general impression made by the show was that the newest and most interesting types of aeroplanes and engines were being held back. However, this is no wonder, given the international situation.
>
> 'It must be admitted that the German exhibit by its location and arrangement dominated the show. As one entered the building the villainous-looking Junkers 87 dive-bomber immediately attracted attention. It was raised well off the floor in a diving attitude.

'Although the showmanship was good, the aeroplane itself was not very impressive or modern and one guesses that it is now obsolescent.'

(... as we would soon see in the blitzkrieg, Mr Stuart?)

'The largest machine at the show was the Vickers Wellington which has a span of 86 feet. ... amazing spectacle of a completely fabric covered large high-speed bomber ... It has been compared to a basket or a crab-pot with gloves on but its speed of 265mph indicates that it is a basket of very special shape and refinement. It was notable as being the only twin-engined type at the show whose wheels completely disappeared behind doors when retracted.'

Despite the annexation by Hitler of Bohemia and Moravia only a few weeks before, the Czech aircraft manufacturer Letov was exhibiting what turned out to be its last type, the Š-50, a general purpose, military twin-engined monoplane, top speed 190mph, with a fixed undercarriage. As Mr Stuart noted, this was unusual at the time for a machine of this size. The Letov factory in Prague spent the war repairing rather more modern machines for the Luftwaffe.

Some of those Belgian officers at the gala dinners must have been members of the escadrilles based at Évere and equipped with Fairey Battles as well as the aerobatic Gloster Gladiators. They would have the chance to fly only one op and be decimated trying to stop the Germans crossing the Albert Canal in May 1940.

At home four more squadrons waited to be restocked with the Wellington – or 'Wimpy' as it was universally known after the character J. Wellington Wimpy in the Popeye cartoons. Harrows made way at 37 Squadron, likewise at 214 with war less than two months away, and at 215 which was promptly reassigned as a training squadron.

The Air Ministry demanded one more display of aerial might – the 'Showing the Wings' initiative when all available Wellingtons of Bomber Command 3 Group would fly over France, 18 July 1939, in formation to Marseilles. That was the intention, at any rate, and they all took off from their home bases and assembled north of London. South of the capital, the weather was worsening and every aircraft was sent instructions to reroute along the English south coast. Further

Wellingtons of 9 Squadron impress the crowds at the Brussels Air Show, Sunday 9 July 1939.

orders to return to base were received by some squadrons before others, resulting in two-way mid-air traffic that would have been even more horrifying for the crews had they been able to see very far.

Only two squadrons, No. 9 and No. 214, were deemed to have shown the discipline and skill required in a large formation and, it must have been noticed, for the daylight air raids to come, and so they were selected to show their wings in a more modest way, a flight of eighteen aircraft going to Marseilles and back the next day.

Another flight to Marseilles on 23 July had formation-keeping as a secondary consideration to petrol consumption. An improvement was noted – from 2.6mpg to 3mpg. This was followed on 5 and 6 August

Also at the Brussels show, despite the annexation by Hitler of Bohemia and Moravia only a few weeks before, the Czech aircraft manufacturer Letov was exhibiting what turned out to be its last type, the Š-50, a general purpose, military twin-engined monoplane, top speed 190mph, with a fixed undercarriage.

The 'villainous-looking' Junkers 87 dive-bomber in attacking pose was the most modern aircraft the Germans chose to show at Brussels in the summer of 1939. All in good time, they might have said, all in good time.

by Bomber Command Tactical Exercises. Those on the 7 August were cancelled because of bad weather. The next three days were devoted to the RAF Annual Home Defence Exercise in which 1,300 aircraft took part, testing the air and ground defences of Great Britain against air attack and the efficiency of the forces engaged.

A line was drawn from Withernsea, Yorkshire, to Bournemouth, Dorset, to provide an area to be defended by anti-aircraft guns, searchlights, balloons, and 800 aircraft – of which 500 were fighters. The attackers were 500 bombers and in the words of the time: 'Their raids were presumed to have come from territories located east of the operational area.' There was to be a full-scale black-out monitored by ARP wardens during the night of 9 10 August, but unsuitable weather postponed it to the following night when it was considered effectively carried out on the whole.

Rain, poor visibility and low clouds frequently interfered with the work of both attackers and defenders, although the attackers seemed to suffer less and many of the bombers reached their targets and were not intercepted. The bombers used the cloud to avoid the fighters, some of which were not allowed to take off in case the weather caused collisions. The anti-aircraft gunners claimed to have hit some of the bombers.

The Air Minister, Sir Kingsley Wood, praised everybody and congratulated all on the most valuable experience gained. He also profoundly regretted the loss of several fine airmen who had met with fatal accidents. And that was that.

Members of the Public Schools OTC visited RAF Calshot in the summer of 1939. Some of them doubtless were destined for Bomber Command but here they are going to lunch. The aircraft behind right is a Short Stranraer flying boat; on the left are two Short Singapores. In time for the war, 201 Squadron was equipped with the Saunders-Roe London flying boat used by Coastal Command for U-boat hunting until mid 1940, replaced by the Sunderland.

'M. Pierre Béranger, vice-president of the Aeronautical Commission, stated that young fighter pilots need a training of at least 150 hours, while bomber pilots require a training of 400 hours.'

L'Air, August 1939.

'Not even gulls will be able to cross the Mediterranean without our permission after the Italo-Spanish air union has been concluded.'

General Kindelan, AOC Spanish Air Force, July 1939.

'Following recent successful experiments, a number of Italian reconnaissance machines will be equipped with television transmission sets enabling them to send off instantaneous pictorial reports of work done. The only problem still awaiting solution concerns the dimensions of the apparatus, which is very heavy.'

L'Aquilone, 13 August 1939.

Sidelight on the Exercises. Personnel were constantly by their machines, even to the extent of eating off them.

Three days of August 1939 were devoted to the RAF Annual Home Defence Exercise, in which 1,300 aircraft took part, to test the air and ground defences of Great Britain against air attack and the efficiency of the forces engaged. All noses to the grindstone.

Get a flying start..

with a Short-Service Commission

Ask yourself these questions. Do you want to be in the vanguard of the finest Air Force in the World? Do you want to benefit yourself *and* your country? And do you want a job that's exciting, interesting and worthwhile? You do? Then the answer is a Short Service Commission in the Royal Air Force. How can you qualify? By being between the ages of 17½ and 28, unmarried, physically fit and educated to School Certificate standard (though an actual certificate is not necessary). When you've qualified you choose whether you'll serve four years—with six further years on the Reserve *and* a gratuity on transfer of £300, or six years—with four years on the Reserve and £500 on transfer. Pay is £340 rising to £520 a year, in cash and kind. And you get very good leave on full pay. Send that coupon off today—*NOW!*

JOIN THE RAF

AIR MINISTRY, (Dept. S7e/PRCI), Kingsway, London.

NAME....................................

Please send me free pamphlet about Short-Service Commissions in the Royal Air Force. (No obligation is entailed.)

ADDRESS....................................

....

Perhaps those OTC boys would clip the coupon from this ad, August 1939.

CHAPTER 2

So. Are we ready?

Unaware of great matters of state and of the aircraft industry – but certainly feeling the wind blowing hard down the streets of the old town of Hull and lashing the winter evening rain into his face – was a tall, thin youth on a bicycle. Standing on the pedals in his efforts against the storm made the chain come off. Over there was a notice: 'No. 8 Centre Royal Air Force Volunteer Reserve'. More important

ANOTHER ONE FOR DR. GOEBBELS' LIBRARY OF WAR PICTURES: *One of Britain's fleet of mighty war 'planes. This monster of the skies flies aloft at nearly 52 m.p.h. and is declared capable of crossing the Channel. Trained aeronauts are in charge of the machines. The principle of the engine is that of internal combustion. Britain now boasts proudly that she has not one steam-driven air-o'-plane left in the Royal Air Force. Her fleet of the up-to-date machines pictured here is upwards of 40. Each pilot is a Master of Arts and has reached the qualified age of 65.*

War is on the Way Number One: this is how one satirist saw the state of preparedness in RAF Bomber Command.

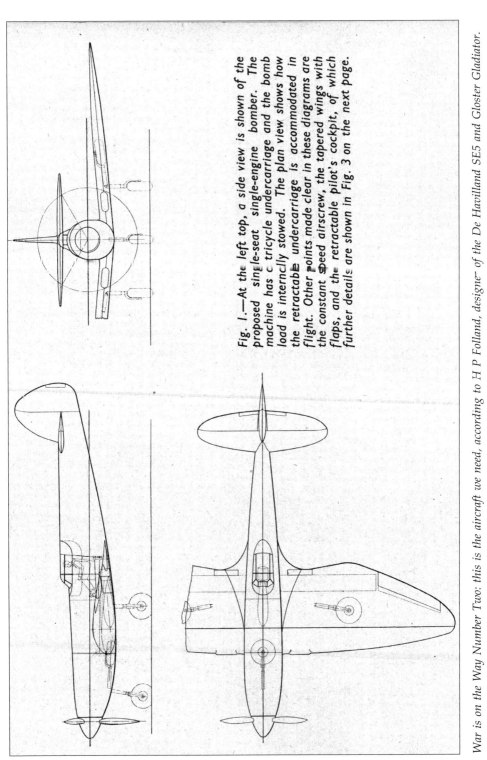

Fig. 1.—At the left top, a side view is shown of the proposed single-seat single-engine bomber. The machine has a tricycle undercarriage and the bomb load is internally stowed. The plan view shows how the retractable undercarriage is accommodated in flight. Other points made clear in these diagrams are the constant speed airscrew, the tapered wings with flaps, and the retractable pilot's cockpit, of which further details are shown in Fig. 3 on the next page.

War is on the Way Number Two: this is the aircraft we need, according to H P Folland, designer of the De Havilland SE5 and Gloster Gladiator.

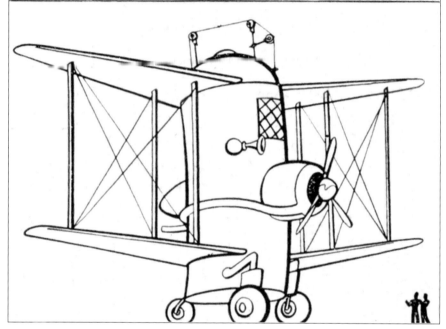

War is on the Way Number Three. Another view of the aircraft we need, September 1939.

was a bright light beyond and the promise of warmth. The youth stood, dripping, in the hallway. A short, slight, balding, clerical sort of chap bounced out of a room: 'Hello. Over eighteen, are you?' he asked.

It was February 1938. Rupert Douglas Cooling – called 'Tiny' because he was 6ft 7in – replied: 'Not till next month, sir.'

'Good, good, excellent,' said the man. 'You look rather wet. Out walking without a mackintosh?'

'On my bicycle, actually. Chain came off. I was ...'

'Good, good, excellent,' said the man. 'There are forms to fill in, of course, then a selection interview and a medical. Eyesight all right?'

'Yes, it's ...'

'Good, good, excellent. That's the main thing. No use as a pilot without it. Now, assuming you get through the formalities, you'll be Aircraftman Second Class … er, didn't catch the name.'

'Cooling, sir. Rupert Cooling. They call me Tiny.'

'AC2 Cooling. Then, in the fastest promotion you will ever have, the next morning you'll be Sergeant Cooling, pilot under training. Such an exalted rank attracts the dignified rate of pay of ten shillings and sixpence per diem rising, upon qualification as the pilot afore-mentioned, to twelve shillings and sixpence.'

'Well, sir, I was thinking about joining the Territorial Army.'

'Good, good, excellent. Very similar. Here we give you fifteen days per annum continuous training, plus weekends and evenings. Full pay for the fifteen days, annual bounty of £25 assuming regular attendance, travelling expenses, and 2s an hour for the lectures and whatnot.'

'Lectures?'

'Things a pilot must know. Theory of flight, navigation, meteorology, armaments, signals, rules and regulations. There's a bar in which to practise beer drinking and Mrs Kirby the caretaker's wife will provide you with beans on toast and a pot of tea beforehand. Stay there a minute. I'll get you the forms.'

With chain fixed and rain stopped, the boy rode home feeling as if he had won the football pools – 10s 6d a day. A day! All he got as an apprentice pharmacist was 10s a week, less 1s 3d for insurance stamps. These fellows gave you two bob an hour for listening to a lecture and twenty-five quid just for turning up. And then there was the flying.

No problems arose – apart from the medical examiner's measuring stick only going up to 6ft 6in – and soon Aircraftman Second Class Cooling was on King George's aerial strength and instantly promoted.

On Sunday 27 March 1938 Sergeant Cooling took the train to Brough where was the factory of the Blackburn Aircraft Company and a flying school. Fitted with Sidcot suit and leather helmet with Bakelite cups over his ears, he was introduced to Flying Officer Morris.

Flying Officer Morris had a truly massive moustache. Years later in the war, Squadron Leader 'Chuff-Chuff' Morris (so named for his habit of blowing through his moustache) would be Officer Com-manding the Aircrew Disciplinary Course, a residential fortnight of light punishment for unruly aircrew. As virtually all aircrew were unruly it was a mystery how penitents were selected.

Teacher and pupil set off across the grass and ignored the superior Hawker Hart trainers for a friendlier Blackburn B2 – a type built in 1931 in a failed bid to rival the De Havilland Tiger Moth. The B2 carried its two airmen, the instructor and the instructed, side by side in the open cockpit. The Tiger Moth had them fore and aft. The Air Ministry decided that training should be in fore and aft mode. Of the forty-two B2s built at Brough, several were still there. Despite the Ministry, Tiny would learn side by side.

Coming out of his Bakelite ear pieces was some braid covered rubber tubing which joined in front to a long single tube. Morris stuck this into a piece of brass pipe which he threaded through his harness so he didn't have to hold it. On the end of the brass pipe was a mask. When Morris spoke into this his voice travelled along the tubes and into Tiny's Bakelite stereo:

'Can you hear me, Sergeant Cooling?'

Tiny nodded. He didn't have a speaking tube so obviously wasn't expected to say anything. Morris pointed to the instruments.

'Engine speed in revs per minute. Oil temperature. Oil pressure. Watch them carefully and often. Air speed indicator calibrated in knots, one hundred absolute top whack downhill, more like eighty usually. Altimeter to tell you how high you are. Turn and bank indicator shows your attitude, wing up, nose down and so on. All right so far?'

Tiny nodded again.

There was a man outside the aircraft dressed in a blue boiler suit. When Flying Officer Morris gave this man the thumbs up, he stepped forward and took hold of the prop.

'Switches off. Suck in,' shouted the man.

'Switches off.' Morris's moustache was escaping from his speaking mask in all directions. 'Throttle open slightly,' he said to Tiny. 'Stick hard back. Tail trim fully back. Look behind or you might blow something over when the engine starts.' He looked to the front again.

'Contact,' called the man in the boiler suit.

'Contact,' replied Morris, and the man grabbed the end of the prop and swung it round sharply in a great clockwise arc. He stepped back sharply as the Gypsy engine caught, fired and roared. Morris throttled back to a contented clucking, checked the gauges, and spoke again through the tube which was almost necessary now the engine was going:

'Rev her up to full power with the stick hard back. There, nineteen hundred rpm. Throttle back ... there, to seventeen, and turn off the magnetos one at a time. You'll get a drop of about fifty rpm for each. If you get more, stop and call the doctor. Right. Everything fine. Off we go. Chocks away.'

The man in the boiler suit pulled away the wheel chocks which were the only brakes the B2 had, and they rolled gently forward as Morris opened the engine up again. There was no runway. Morris headed for the furthest downwind point of the field:

'Flying aircraft have precedence over those on the ground, so first you must make certain that nobody is coming in to land. Over the field is the circuit, an invisible and flexible circular pathway. At the moment there's no one on it. So, turn into the wind, centre the tail.' Such was air traffic control.

Morris kept up a commentary. 'Slowly but steadily advance the throttle. Stick forward to lift the tail. Sliding about a bit at forty knots, now the rudder bites, keep her straight, let the stick come back. At fifty knots, she wants to fly. Hold her level, up to sixty-five, ease the stick back.'

There was no doubt about it. They were flying.

Look at that, down there. It was the airfield. It wasn't grass any more, just greenness. How flat everything looked. It was a model village, a mosaic of roofs and streets. Almost every chimney had smoke coming from it, strands of grey wool all stretching in the same direction, pointing to where they, the flying men, had been.

Tiny was hooked. Henceforth there was no possibility of anything else. He was going to be a pilot in the RAF.

This RAF now had some aircraft capable of attacking targets in Germany. There were nowhere near enough for an all-out war nor, including Rupert Cooling and those like him, were there men to fly them should there ever be enough, or yet a cohesive system for fully training such men. There were no navigation aids beyond the old methods of map, compass, landmarks, stars and dead reckoning to help crews find their targets in bad weather or at night. There was no stratagem of aircraft combining together to hit a marked target and no devices for target marking had there been a stratagem. Worse, there had been no serious thinking about how these matters might be resolved.

The idea that bombers could defend themselves successfully against enemy fighters had not been tried, much less proved and, Wellingtons apart, there were surely no war-winners among the rest of Bomber Command's equipment, even though a full-scale offensive of strategic bombing against Germany was the official policy.

Air Chief Marshal Sir Edgar Ludlow-Hewitt, Commander-in-Chief of the bomber force, had had a brilliant career in the first war, starting as a pilot of high repute and ending as a thirty-one-year-old brigadier, Royal Flying Corps. That he had a superb brain and exceptional talent for administration and analysis was never in doubt, though his abilities as a front-line commander were less apparent to some of his senior colleagues.

He was appointed to the top bomber job in 1937 and all the facts as outlined above soon became horribly obvious to him. His pleas for more resources did not resonate loudly enough with the Air Ministry which was preoccupied, as most officials and politicians were, with the requirements of Fighter Command. In any case, there was that general belief, summed up years before by Stanley Baldwin, that the bombers would always get through. There was also opposition, or inertia, among those who objected to the whole business of bombing a country into submission. The RAF's plan for destroying industrial targets in the Ruhr was initially met with a ministerial objection that factories were private property.

Ludlow-Hewitt saw that if he were asked to mount that offensive, Bomber Command would be totally destroyed. He calculated that his current force would be annihilated within eight weeks. That force consisted of fifty-three squadrons of five types of aircraft – Wellington, Whitley, Hampden, Blenheim and Battle.

His realistic assessment was reluctantly accepted but he was viewed as a pessimist and, probably, despite his cold and distant demeanour, too soft-hearted to be a warlord. He would soon be replaced. Meanwhile, ten squadrons of Battles were scheduled for France and the so-called Advanced Air Striking Force, and a message from President Roosevelt urged the future combatants, Britain, France and Germany, to exercise restraint in the use of their bombers and to avoid civilian casualties. Not wishing to offend the Americans, Britain and France agreed right away and Germany too a few weeks later, once it became unnecessary to bomb Poland.

' "The invisible wall", the Air Defence Zone West, is unsurpassable. Raiding machines will either be brought down entering German territory, or leaving it.'

German periodical Der Adler, 22 August 1939.

'Large industrial plants of the Ruhr district are protected by 30 and more balloons which, in case of stronger winds, are replaced by kites.'

Der Adler, 22 August 1939.

'Anti-aircraft defence in National Socialist Germany is no longer a technical problem; it is a spiritual one. It proves the maturity of a nation which knows its destiny is in excellent hands.'

A German newspaper waxes philosophical about the defence of Berlin, 1 September 1939.

For the time being the British and the French found the Roosevelt stricture convenient. The French greatly feared a bomber war, having an air force, mostly equipped with obsolete aircraft, quite unable to resist. The RAF could not fly bomber missions from the UK over neutral Belgium and The Netherlands – or over France for that matter – so attacks on Germany would require some circuitous routing.

The great bomber offensive was off. Twenty of Bomber Command's squadrons were assigned to training roles.

Mobilisation of Bomber Command was ordered on 1 September 1939. Most of the squadrons of Battles flew to France on 2 September. One of 40 Squadron had engine failure and had to ditch; the crew were rescued. The rest arrived at their grass airfields, some of which were improvised to say the least, and set about hiding their presence. The plan had nothing to do with defending and repelling any German invasion of France, an event not yet considered likely. Rather, the AASF's light bombers were indeed meant to strike, and to strike into Germany from a more convenient distance should the enemy start bombing Britain. That this was an entirely mad idea must have occurred to almost everyone but it went ahead anyway.

So, on this day, Saturday 2 September 1939, Bomber Command had twenty-three squadrons as the entire UK-based operational force, the shield in question, being six of Wellingtons, six each of Hampdens and Blenheims, and five of Whitleys, while the Luftwaffe could attack Poland with 900 bombers and dive bombers.

The Blenheims could not be considered serious bombers for attacks on Germany, so we can count seventeen squadrons capable of taking a worthwhile quantity of bombs to enemy territory and coming home again, roughly 170 aircraft serviceable and ready at any given moment.

Enemy territory, in the sense of targets on land, was forbidden so only the German navy was a legitimate aiming point, provided it was at sea. If it was in harbour civilians might be hit, but out on the ocean, well, Mr Roosevelt could not object to that. To find and hit warships, operations would have to be in daylight, so that let the Whitleys off the hook but brought the Blenheims back into the reckoning. There

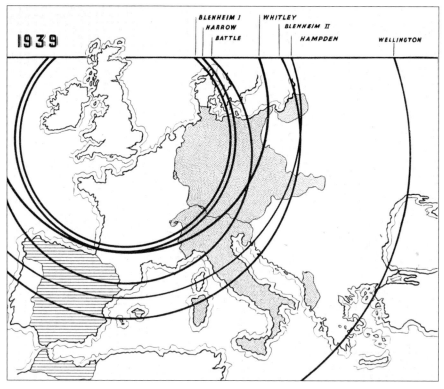

An expert, Captain Norman Macmillan MC, AFC, ponders the possibilities of Bomber Command, showing the potential of the various aircraft when operational, that is, carrying a useful bomb-load. 'The radius of action shown allows for windage, deflection of course due to enemy action, storms, etc.'

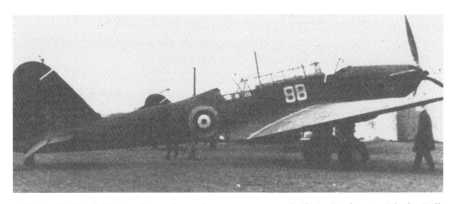

A Fairey Battle of 88 Squadron, shown here pre-war, was built in Stockport with the Rolls Royce Merlin engine. In performance trials, the Battle made 210mph at 16,200ft and flew 1,050 miles with a full bomb load of 1,000lb.

It had a good reputation as being easy to fly, with reasonable comfort and forward vision for the pilot but poor rear vision, which was where the fighters often came from.

would be no fighter escorts despite Ludlow-Hewitt saying they were essential, because the RAF did not have fighters with sufficient range to reach the areas where the warships currently were stationed.

On the morning of Sunday 3 September at 11.15am, war was publicly declared on the BBC by Prime Minister Chamberlain speaking to you

Fairey Battles of 218 Squadron – K9325 (furthest) was shot down attacking German troops at St Vith, Belgium, crew taken prisoner; K9353 (nearest) was shot down over Luxembourg, 12 May 1940, all crew killed. K9324 was a very rare 218 bird – it survived.

> 'Our first line strength is already well over 1,750 machines, which means that we can keep that formidable number in the air almost indefinitely, whatever the losses.
>
> 'And I hear that a new long-range, fast bomber is being developed, capable of looking after itself in all circumstances, and of carrying the war very far indeed into the enemy's camp.'
>
> Ray Norman, Parliamentary Correspondent,
> *Aeronautics*, August 1939.
>
> 'The total number of entries (to the RAF) of pilots, observers, airmen and boys during the period April 1–July 1 1939 was 12,265, as compared with 4,676 for the corresponding period in 1938.'
>
> Air Ministry announcement.

from the Cabinet Room at number ten Downing Street and saying that no such undertaking had been received and that consequently this country was at war with Germany.

The expectation in Bomber Command was probably all-out war with squadrons on a three-week cycle: maximum effort one week, sustained effort (roughly half speed) one week, rest one week. The Luftwaffe was not thought to be as good a fighting force as the RAF even though it was numerically vastly superior.

> 'Fog landings may be made easier for air line pilots by the installation of the landing strip, lit by coloured lights, that was started at Croydon last month. The device consists of two parallel strips containing coloured lamps set flush with the aerodrome surface, with colours arranged in sequence to indicate the various lengths of the run illuminated. Heston has had such a landing strip in operation for some time.'
>
> *Aeronautics* magazine 'News of the Month', August 1939.
>
> 'Snack bar trolleys, laden with pies, cakes, biscuits and cups of tea, are sent round the works of Leyland Motors, Ltd., twice a day to supply light refreshments to the workers at their benches.'
>
> *Aeronautics* magazine 'News of the Month', August 1939.

Less than an hour after Mr Chamberlain finished his speech, an attempt was made to carry the fight to the enemy by the only means possible. There were great hopes for a naval blockade of Germany but obviously that wasn't on station yet, so it had to be by air. The offensive against the Third Reich began with a single Blenheim Mark IV number N6125 of 139 Squadron, captained by a twenty-one-year-old Glasgow boy, Flying Officer Andrew McPherson, and sent from RAF Wyton across the sea towards Wilhelmshaven to reconnoitre ship movements.

The crew of three – pilot, wireless operator/gunner and a naval officer as observer to identify the ships – flew through cloud and icy conditions but, close to their limit at 24,000 feet, found what they were looking for – a large contingent of the German navy, capital ships and destroyer escorts, in the Schillig Roads, steaming north from Wilhelmshaven towards Heligoland. Delighted with their success, Corporal Arrowsmith telegraphed the news on his Morse key but his equipment was frozen.

The wireless sets they all had were difficult to tune (it had to be done manually) and were not properly insulated against the cold, to which they were very susceptible, so communication between aircraft and base was often lost, especially at long distance. Arrowsmith's message was not understood.

Vincent Arrowsmith, promoted to sergeant – the minimum rank for aircrew after mid-1940 – would be killed in another 139 Squadron Blenheim, 24 September 1940, attacking shipping in the English Channel, by which time his skipper was also dead (*see Chapter Six*).

McPherson and crew – the first to fly into what amounted to enemy airspace – landed home in the early afternoon and passed on the message the old-fashioned way. The squadrons on standby had had their lunch and had more or less given up hope of an attack when the news came through. It was late, too late really to contemplate a mission with a healthy outcome, but the orders were clear: three Hampdens of 49 Squadron and six of 83, all based at Scampton, and six Wellingtons of 37 (Feltwell) and three of 149 (Mildenhall) were to take off on 'armed reconnaissance'.

Among the pilots at 83 Squadron was Flying Officer Guy Gibson, on this day a confused novitiate. Four 500lb bombs with a delayed fuse of 11.5 seconds had been put aboard his and all the other Hampdens so that they could go in low to bomb without blowing themselves up in the consequent blast. Take-off would be at 15.30 hours; first, the briefing.

Gibson, in his book *Enemy Coast Ahead*, has this operation on the second day of the war, 4 September. He admits to writing without notes and without a diary so we must allow him a memory lapse. There is no doubt that the op occurred on 3 September. Gibson:

> 'To call it a briefing would be absurd. We all gathered around a table while the Station Commander (Group Captain Emmett) told us where we were going. "You are to attack the German pocket battleships in the Schillig Roads at the entrance to the Kiel Canal. If by any chance there are no warships there, you may bomb the ammunition depot at Marienhof but on no account must you bomb civilian establishments, either houses or dockyards."'

The Group Captain went on to explain that the weather would be foul and there had been reports of balloons, but they wouldn't be seen because they'd be in the clouds. The squadrons were not to hang around long, and were not to press home the attack if it couldn't be done according to plan.

The squadron commanders now outlined the plan. As they approached, a battleship would be selected as the target and they would spread out and attack from three directions. To avoid their bombs bouncing off the armoured decks, they were to try and lodge them in the superstructure. Their best height would be 3,000 feet – above machine-gun fire but below heavy flak. On the journey there and back, on no account were they to break formation and act as individuals. Gibson:

> 'Another fellow got up and told us how to take off with a bomb load on. None of us had ever done it before and we didn't even know whether our Hampdens would unstick with two thousand pounds of bombs. The advice we got was to ease them off by working the tail trimmer tabs after the tail had come up. If we were still on the ground when the hedge came along we were to yank back the stick as hard as we could and pull the emergency boost control.'

The opportunity to try this was postponed to 16.00 and, after another tiresome and nerve-jangling delay, take-off was finally confirmed as 17.00. Gibson:

'By now we were very nervous; in fact, my hands were shaking so much I couldn't hold them still. Most of us went to the lavatory about four times an hour.'

He might have added that it was now going to be dark when they got back, and coming home from Germany over the sea at night could have been added to 'none of us had ever done it before'.

Gibson, of course, was writing retrospectively, having experienced many more structured briefings with an intelligence officer telling crews about the main aiming point and the alternatives should they not find it, and the severity of the defences they might encounter. A signals officer would give details of the radio beacons identifying home airfields, and the colours of the day to be fired from a Very pistol in the event of friendly attack. There would be more gen about bomb loads and fuel loads, and the weather forecast.

The poor met officer was regarded as a bit of a joke. He never seemed to get it right. He would make brave attempts to forecast cloud cover and wind direction and speed, there and back, but he had so little hard data to work from that he was not doing much more than guessing.

The wind was very important in a flight, and there was no means of measuring its effects accurately from the bomber. In a strong crosswind, for instance, an aircraft behaved like a boat on a swiftly flowing river, heading for a specific point on the far bank but constantly drifting off course and having to make corrections. Any small difference in the expected wind (the wind by which the navigator made his calculations), and the actual wind could have fatal consequences if the difference was not noticed. The only reliable way of noticing was to see pinpoints on the ground, so this was a problem frequently unsolved.

Take-off times were allocated but, in these early years, captain and observer (the RAF term for navigator at the time) decided their own route and height, noting landmarks on their charts that would help them to stay on track.

Regardless of being without modern conveniences on the first day of the war 83 Squadron got away without too much trouble and tried to settle in to the job in hand. Gibson:

> 'The aeroplane felt very heavy. It was some time before we picked up any speed at all, her turns were sluggish and she tended to slip inwards. I could not believe that I was leaving England to go to Germany to carry out an act of war.'

Crossing the coast near Skegness, with the Butlin's holiday camp clearly seen below, they drummed over the sea for two hours at about 1,000 feet, passing over a Dornier 18 flying boat that they could have attacked, but did not. Nearing the Heligoland Bight, they flew into bad weather:

> 'The cloud suddenly descended to about three hundred feet in rain. I had to open the window, getting very wet, to see Willy (Snaith, flight leader) at all.'

They could see what looked like gunfire ahead. With the cloud now down to 100 feet, Snaith turned and led his men away. They could have been miles off track, had no idea what was firing at what, and being so low made sighting any ships even less likely. There was no chance of attacking according to plan.

The Handley Page Hampden first flew in 1936 and entered service in 1938, and it was still bombing Germany in 1941. This one, L4045 EA/Q-Queenie of 49 Squadron, had a long and distinguished war career, putting in almost 800 operational flying hours. After an attack on the battleship Tirpitz, *11/12 January 1941, L4045 crashed at Scampton base, killing all four crew. Q-Queenie was already known around the stations as the one that got lost and landed, out of petrol, on The Curragh racecourse, Dublin, in May 1940, when it was swiftly given enough fuel to hop over into Northern Ireland.*

In the murk, the crews of 49 Squadron thought they spotted the Horns Rev (Reef) lightship, which was off the Danish shore about seventy-five miles north-east of Heligoland. They too turned for home.

The Wellington crews found nothing either but they had at least flown to Germany and back in daylight, without mishap, and this was taken at HQ as evidence that Wellingtons were day bombers. This belief would have catastrophic results later in the year.

Having risked their lives for nothing on a mission that was bound to fail, at least the war's first raiders did all return. Last home, after midnight, were the three Hampdens of Gibson's flight, the leader's navigator having got lost over Lincolnshire and been unable to find any directions until the moon came up and landmarks were visible

From the enemy's point of view, the only sign of war so far had been a single scout flying too high to worry about.

None of this made it into the newspapers, but another raid would. While the Hampdens and Wellingtons were coming home, some more experienced night-flying men were heading for Germany. Seven Whitleys of 58 Squadron and three of 51 set off from Linton-on-Ouse. Some were briefed to head for the industrial cities in the Ruhr, going the long way over France to avoid neutral Belgium and The Netherlands, and some via the Heligoland Bight to Hamburg and other targets in northern Germany. In years to come, bombers in their hundreds would arrive at one target and drop thousands of tons of bombs in half an hour. In September 1939 nobody knew the first thing about how to bomb Germany and so the traditional method of leaving it to the captains to choose their targets from a selection provided and their own routes there and back was used.

As they didn't know themselves, we cannot know whether those Whitley crews arrived precisely at their destinations, but they certainly reached Germany and reported searchlights believed to be at Hamburg and Bremen, and generally in the Ruhr region. We can also say that they attacked the enemy in several different places with millions of weapons doing no damage whatsoever. The weapons were leaflets telling the Germans to stop it now – or words to that effect.

There would be many such raids, having no discernible effect on their targets but causing losses to Bomber Command. The leaflets were known as 'nickels', and the activity 'nickelling', but quite why is not known although there are several unsubstantiated theories.

There was certainly a curious perception among senior commanders that leaflet raids were somehow less dangerous than bombing raids. As the war developed, the job was often given to crews still in training. In the sense that there was no great pressure to find a specific target and so need to hang around in heavily defended areas, nickelling was a way to initiate bomber crews into ops although the men didn't think much of it. They wanted to drop bombs, not paper. Anyway, as one gunner recalled, the high-altitude winds were sometimes so strong that the leaflets would be back in the UK before he was.

Three of the Whitley crews could not find their way home before their petrol ran out and had to crash land in France. Two preserved themselves and their machines in doing so. One, Whitley Mark III K8969 GE-G of 58 Squadron, captained by Flying Officer J. A. O'Neill, came down in the dawn light in a field of cabbages on the banks of the River Marne, some twenty miles or so from Reims. The crew were unhurt but the aircraft became Bomber Command's first loss of the war.

The Armstrong Whitworth Whitley was front-line equipment in 1939 and made the first night-time raids over Germany, carrying leaflets. Known as the flying barn door, it had this curious nose-down attitude in flight and, compared with the Wellington and Luftwaffe fighters, it was obsolete before it went into action.

The tools were primitive for navigation. They had maps, of course, and time pieces. The compass was more or less reliable except in stormy weather when lightning and static electricity affected it, but it was only useful if you knew where you were. As the Irishman said when asked directions, 'if I were you I wouldn't start from here'.

The air speed indicator could freeze up. Home-based radio stations could sometimes get a fix on a lost aircraft which might be received if the wireless was working well. So, if a crew couldn't see anything to help, their dead reckoning relied on sources of information that could all be wrong – air speed, wind speed and direction and compass readings. Some crews carried a sextant which could give general assistance in a cloudless sky. And when you did get back to base, your aerodrome and all the others nearby might be shrouded in fog.

A flight commander at 102 Squadron, Squadron Leader Morris, put it this way:

'Each captain planned his own route to the target. Bombing tactics likewise were delegated. A take-off time was laid down but if you were delayed you still went so long as you had enough time to come back over the enemy coast before daylight. Because there were no navigation aids it was all done by dead reckoning and looking at the ground and so navigation was poor. Some captains distrusted their observers and decided on course alterations themselves. The result was a great many losses due to running out of petrol while many miles off track on the way home. At the interrogation when you did get home, the intelligence officers didn't like it if you admitted you were not sure if you'd been to the target laid down. They gave you a black mark. Tired and jumpy crews got wise to this and said "O yes, hit the jolly target bob on", and slid away to bed early.'

On the second day, 4 September, the papers published instructions about recognising air-raid warnings and what to do when one heard them. Milkmen, coalmen and other drivers of horse-drawn vehicles were to tether their animals to the nearest tree or lamppost before seeking shelter. The signal for poison gas would be hand rattles to say it's here, and hand bells to say it's been cleared away. Adults should identify children 'able to run about' by writing names and addresses on luggage labels and attaching same where they could not be removed.

All cinemas, theatres and other places of entertainment were to be closed immediately until further notice because large numbers of people would be killed if such places were hit by bombs. The same applied to sports gatherings (Yorkshire had already won the County Championship for the third year in succession) and 'all gatherings for purposes of entertainment or amusement, whether outdoor or indoor. Churches and other places of public worship will not be closed.'

Announcements from the department stores encouraged people to buy now while stocks lasted. Debenham and Freebody had 'in the inexpensive department a number of attractive early autumn frocks at reasonable prices' that were 'likely to prove of use to busy women at the present time' and were 'easy to get into quickly'. Coal, gas and electricity went on the ration at seventy-five per cent of that used by consumers in the previous year. Controls on petrol would be much more strictly applied.

According to *The Times* on this Monday morning London showed 'quiet and resolute preparedness for whatever may come. Overhead were the innumerable barrage balloons, gleaming like beads of quick-silver, serene and beautiful, against a background of blue sky and cotton-wool clouds.'

The weather was not so good over northern Germany, which forced Flying Officer McPherson in a repeat of his first trip, and according to his *London Gazette* DFC citation, 'to fly close to the enemy coast at very low altitudes' in his early-morning reconnaissance Blenheim. He managed to spot naval units anchored offshore near Brunsbüttel, a small harbour town of Schleswig-Holstein near the Danish border, population around 7,000, and at Wilhelmshaven, population 118,000. The populations were safe but Brunsbüttel was an important naval base on the Elbe estuary, the western terminus of the Kiel Canal and sixty miles downstream from Hamburg. Wilhelmshaven was the chief naval base for all the North Sea fleet, with ten harbour basins and six dry docks and currently, the battleship *Admiral Scheer*, with destroyers and cruisers nearby including the training cruiser *Emden*.

Yet again, the wireless message was not understood and so orders to mount an attack were not issued until the middle of the day after McPherson got back. The orders came from HQ of 2 Group of Bomber Command, for five Blenheims of each of 107, 110, and 139 Squadrons to fly to Wilhelmshaven, and from 3 Group for six Wellingtons of 9 Squadron and eight of 149 to fly to Brunsbüttel.

The briefings for all the squadrons were unusual enough, being the first of their kind any of the men, the briefers and the briefed, had ever been to, but with the addition of a message from King George VI:

> 'The Royal Air Force has behind it a tradition no less inspiring than those of the older Services, and in the campaign which we have now been compelled to undertake you will have to assume responsibilities far greater than those which your Service had to shoulder in the last war. I can assure all ranks of the air force of my supreme confidence in their skill and courage, and in their ability to meet whatever calls may be made upon them.'

Whether or not they had much idea about the reality of the calls being made upon them, there can be no doubt that the King's message, welcomed though it must have been, was entirely unnecessary as motivation.

Squadron Leader Lennox Lamb, a New Zealander, would be leading the 9 Squadron men. Of his briefing, he reported that: 'I was ordered to carry out a bombing raid on warships inside Brunsbüttel harbour.' Squadron Leader Paul Harris was ordered to do the same job for 149 Squadron but his account indicates no more briefing than that. After a twenty-four-hour standby, the take-off was frantic, more like a fighter-squadron scramble than a planned bombing raid. The target for 149 was given as warships in the Kiel Canal, and Harris set off in front of his flight without any idea about how to get there or, indeed, just where it was.

The scheme for the Blenheims was much the same as the one for the Hampdens the day before except they would carry two 500-pounders each, with 11.5 second delay fuses. They would go in low in their squadron groups and attack from different directions. 'Low' meant that the bombs – armour-piercing types needing to be dropped from a good height – had to be changed for general purpose ones, causing more frustration for the crews.

The weather worsened as they flew over the sea with mist, rain and low cloud, 'a solid wall of cloud from sea level to 17,000 feet', according to 110 Squadron's leader, acting Flight Lieutenant Ken

King George VI
was a keen visitor
of RAF stations,
when he wore the
uniform of Marshal
of the Royal Air
Force.

Doran. The five Blenheims of 139 Squadron went badly off track, could not find the target, jettisoned their bombs and turned back. At least that meant the five of 110 Squadron had surprise on their side as they spotted the *Admiral Scheer* and went in led by Doran. To find the battleship after flying almost blind was 'an incredible combination of luck and judgement' in Doran's opinion. To quote from his DFC citation:

> 'In face of heavy gun fire and under extremely bad weather conditions he pressed home a successful low attack with great determination.'

In truth, he didn't have the heavy gunfire at first. The sailors on the battleship were said to have 'looked up as if watching an airshow' while Doran's flight hit the *Admiral Scheer* with three or four bombs, one sticking, the others bouncing off, and one near-missing in the water next to the ship, but none of them exploded. Later at home, Doran would give an interview describing the raid in which he produced the line that made him famous:

> 'We could see a German warship taking on stores from two tenders at her stern. We could even see some washing hanging over the rails. Undaunted by the washing we proceeded to bomb the battleship. Flying at 100 feet above mast height all three aircraft in the flight converged on her. I flew straight ahead. The pilot of the second aircraft came across from one side, and the third crossed from the other side. When we flew over the top of the battleship we could see the crews running fast to their stations. We dropped our bombs and hit bang amidships. As we came round, the ship's pom-poms began to fire and the shore batteries opened up. Taking evasive action, we headed for home. My navigator saw shells bursting almost on the tail of the aircraft.'

The tale of Doran's washing went round the RAF messes in short order, with various jokes about catching the Germans with their pants down, but there was a more serious side to the story. While one of the 110 five had strayed and couldn't find the target, with surprise gone the navy gunners set about the fourth to attack, captained by Flying

Officer Henry Emden. It flipped sideways and crashed into the pilot's namesake, the training cruiser *Emden* killing a number of sailors (said to be nine) and, with an extra man on board, all four aircrew.

Now it was 107 Squadron's turn and, again, one aircraft was not present, presumed off track somewhere. The four crews that did go in must have known what was likely to be their fate. The German machine- and flak-gunners were highly accomplished at their trade and there were many of them, in ship and shore batteries. The Blenheims flew right into their fire.

Exactly what happened is not certain. One Blenheim, captained by Flight Lieutenant Bill Barton, went down in the harbour, probably hit by the guns of the *Admiral Hipper*. Either Pilot Officer William Murphy (from County Cork) and crew or Flying Officer Herbert Lightoller and crew, were blown up by their own bomb exploding as it hit a warship – identity and extent of damage unknown – the other aircraft being shot down. The fourth, skippered by Canadian sergeant pilot Albert Prince, was disabled and forced to ditch in the harbour, its pilot later dying of his wounds while the two crew, Sergeant Booth and Aircraftman First Class Slattery, became the first prisoners of the war.

The body of one of the fourteen dead, Sergeant Ray Grossey, Emden's extra man on secondment from 42 Squadron, was never found. The rest were given full military funerals by the Germans.

At Wattisham, the base for 110 and 107, Doran and three more of his flight landed with no sign as yet of 107. At last, with its bombs still on board, a single Blenheim flew in. Ten had set off; five had come home. If this was to be the pattern for Bomber Command, the life of aircrew was likely to be very short.

Booth was traduced into a radio interview for German propaganda. It was a very brief affair with one of the questions about the food he was being given. Any propaganda value was immediately lost for anyone who knew RAF sergeants' mess meals, as he replied with, as it sounded, a perfectly straight face, that the food was wonderful, just like home.

However, the raid had provided the British public with the first heroes of the war. The Ministry of Information reported that the Blenheim pilots and crews were 'proud to have been chosen to strike the first blow at the German war machine.' The DFCs awarded to Andrew McPherson and Kenneth Doran were obviously the war's first medals.

War is here. This is a view of the Kiel raid, 4 September 1939, by Blenheims of 107 and 110 Squadrons, as seen by The Times. F/Lt Ken Doran's washing has already entered the folklore of Bomber Command.

The Wellingtons had taken off around four o'clock as had the Blenheims. Squadron Leader Harris, happier now that his navigator Sergeant Austin had a route plotted on the charts he just happened to have had with him, ordered his guns to be tested. None of them worked. He decided to carry on but lack of practice in formation flying was reducing his strength. Two of his flight fell out of line and could not find their way back in, so jettisoned their bombs and came home. Three more were beaten by the foul weather and also turned back.

Harris's section also broke up in the cloud. With his two wingmen invisible, Harris headed for the target. He was about thirty miles to the north of it when his machine was hit by flak from a ship, causing damage to the already useless rear turret. He jettisoned his bombs and gave up the mission just as his wingmen already had, although one of them was to cause a great deal more furore than the rest of 149 that day, when he dropped his bombs on Denmark.

Number 9 Squadron, based at Honington, a grass airfield off the Ixworth/Thetford road in Suffolk, had proved its ability in formation flying while showing the wings over France and, despite the weather that had caused 149 so much trouble, found Brunsbüttel.

Wellingtons L4268 piloted by Flight Sergeant Ian Borley and L4275 piloted by Flight Sergeant John Turner were the wingmen in Squadron Leader Lamb's section of three. Flight Lieutenant Peter Grant led the other section with another Turner, Flying Officer Robert Turner beside him as second pilot. Sergeants Tom Purdy and Charles Bowen were Grant's wingmen.

By the standards of Bomber Command later in the war, these pilots were old men. Until recently they had been used to flying biplanes, Heyfords, and to a settled, regular RAF life. They were mostly married. Sergeant Borley was thirty and had been a pilot on No. 9 since 1933 when he'd been flying the Vickers Virginia. Lamb, twenty-nine, was similar, although some of the crews were not so venerable, especially the gunners. Despite the strategy of self-defending aircraft, gunnery had yet to be regarded as a specialised trade. Gunners were often ground-crew volunteers, keen young lads who were desperate to do their bit and go a-flying. Flight Sergeant Turner had Aircraft-man Second Class Ken Day, aged twenty. One of Borley's gunners, Leading Aircraftman Harry Dore, was nineteen.

The two section leaders, Lamb and Grant, carried the full crew of six that included the extra side and/or dustbin gunner. Their wingmen had the usual crew of five: pilot, second pilot, observer/navigator, wireless operator/gunner, gunner, except either Borley or Flight Sergeant Turner also had an extra man, Sergeant Heslop, who is not mentioned anywhere except on the Runnymede Memorial and Commonwealth War Graves Commission records.

Grant's section took off at 15.40. Less than three hours later they were in among it. This is his report:

> 'The bombs were dropped at 18.12 hrs at a Battleship which was at a point about ⅞ of a mile due south of the entrance to Kiel. Height 6,000 feet. Immediately after the release we were forced to pull up into the cloud owing to the very high concentration of anti-aircraft fire and turned for home without waiting to see the results. The shore batteries had three or four guns which were firing with far less accuracy than the ships. Six or eight cruisers were firing at us as well as the battleship. We were hit three times. All three machines dropped their bombs at the same time.'

As to battleships, the *Gneisenau* and the *Scharnhorst* were both there.

Lamb's section was up later, at 16.05. By the time they arrived at Brunsbüttel the local *Staffel* of Messerschmitt 109s was ready and waiting. The best bomber the RAF had was about to meet the best fighter in the Luftwaffe – nine of them. Lamb's report showed the normal RAF-officer restraint while describing desperate measures:

> 'Towards the end of a fighter attack carried out by nine German fighters at approx 18.35 I jettisoned my three bombs "live and in stick" at 400 feet on the south side of the harbour. At the moment of bombing I felt sure there was no shipping in the vicinity but having pressed the bomb release I saw a merchant ship, approx 7,000 tons, athwartships. I climbed rapidly, still being attacked by fighters and succeeded in reaching cloud cover. It was necessary for the safety of my crew that these bombs were jettisoned as the decreased load enabled the machine to successfully evade the attack.'

He hit the merchant ship and set it on fire, and his co-pilot, South African Flying Officer Peter Torkington-Leech, manning one of the gun positions – presumably while the designated gunner was firing from the dustbin turret – claimed to have shot down one of the fighters. This claim was not substantiated, so probably there was non-fatal damage inflicted.

The worry expressed earlier, about how groups of bombers might stay together to defend themselves while under fire, was now well illustrated.

Lamb says he was at 400 feet. German reports back this up although there is some confusion in aircraft identification. One fighter pilot said he saw three Wellingtons flying very low over the sea and came at them from above and behind. Two sheered off into the clouds. We must assume that one, either Borley's or Flight Sergeant Turner's, flew on and was shot down in flames because no crew member had seen the German. Another pilot of the same *Gruppe*, II/JG77 (*Jagdgeschwader*, fighter wing) based at Nordholz, near Cuxhaven, stated that he saw another lone Wellington, either Turner's or Borley's, and shot it down.

The Luftwaffe War Diaries have *Feldwebel* (Sergeant) Alfred Held taking 'the Wellington by surprise before its pilot could reach cloud cover' and *Feldwebel* Hans Troitsch bringing down a Blenheim soon afterwards.

No Blenheims fell to fighters that day. Troitsch's victory was the second Wellington – or the first, depending on which version of events is correct. Held was given the credit at the time as the first victor, although he attacked an aircraft on its own while Troitsch later claimed to have seen three together, which must have been before they bombed. Regardless of the primacy claims of Troitsch and Held, there can be no doubt that, as the squadron Operations Record Book reported, 'Nos 2 and 3 of No. 1 Section did not return to base'.

None of the bodies of Borley's crew were found which suggests that his was the aircraft downed by Held out at sea rather than the one destroyed before the attack was made on the ships. Flight Sergeant Turner's body and those of two of his crew were found.

Eleven men, including the unlisted Sergeant Alexander Heslop, were dead at Brunsbüttel, and another fourteen at Wilhelmshaven. Two more were POWs. Of the twenty-nine aircraft setting out on this raid, fifteen never found the target and seven were shot down, leaving only seven that attacked and came home.

The return on this investment was nine (probably) German sailors killed and presumably some injured, no damage to the target ships, some damage to the training cruiser *Emden* and possibly to another warship, and to a merchant ship; little damage to the Luftwaffe.

The Ministry of Information issued a communiqué that night:

> 'A successful attack was carried out during this afternoon by units of the Royal Air Force on vessels of the German Fleet at Wilhelmshaven and at Brunsbüttel, at the entrance of the Kiel Canal.
>
> 'Several direct hits with heavy bombs were registered on a German battleship in the Schilling (sic) Roads, off Wilhelmshaven, which resulted in severe damage.
>
> 'At Brunsbüttel an attack was carried out on a battleship lying alongside the Mole, causing heavy damage. During the operation, which was carried out in very unfavourable weather conditions, our aircraft encountered air attack and anti-aircraft fire, resulting in some casualties.'

The German news agency gave a shorter version. It said that of twelve British bombers which carried out a raid at six o'clock, five were brought down by anti-aircraft batteries. German wireless broadcast their interview with the POW, showing that the enemy propaganda machine was ahead of the game. A BBC broadcast with one of the returning pilots was cancelled.

The Danish government protested that a bomb or bombs had fallen on Esbjerg causing damage to Danish lives and property. The British apologised, 'with profound regret for a most unfortunate incident.' They added:

> 'The captains of all aircraft engaged in the attack on the German Fleet had detailed and stringent instructions to respect Danish neutrality, and the aircraft carried specially trained observers to ensure that only the German warships were attacked.
>
> 'From the most stringent inquiries made it is certain that no aircraft which returned was responsible, but some did not return.

'The attack was carried out in very bad weather, and the aircraft were subsequently engaged in combat above the clouds. One of the missing machines may, therefore, have lost its bearings and unloaded its bombs in the belief that it was over the sea.'

That the 149 Squadron Wellington had lost its bearings cannot be doubted, but it wasn't missing.

The Ministry of Information later issued 'a fairly full account' of this, the first active operation of the RAF in the war:

'The attack was pressed home with the greatest vigour and daring. The fighting qualities displayed by RAF pilots were splendid. The results they achieved are of the highest importance. The navigation of the squadrons was accurate and as they approached the naval bases they flew low to make sure of hitting their targets.

'From the naval point of view their attack will have its effect upon the future course of the war at sea, as the ship hit was one of the most effective units of the German Navy.'

German reports indicated that the ship in question was the *Gneisenau*, which had been bombed but not hit.

Beside this news was the report of the earlier Whitley leaflet raid:

'Aircraft of the Royal Air Force carried out extensive recon-naissance over Northern and Western Germany. They were not engaged by enemy aircraft. More than 6,000,000 copies of a note to the German people were dropped over a wide area.'

Bomber Command's next loss required no Ministry spin doctors to amplify its importance. A Canadian pilot on 7 Squadron, Pilot Officer Anthony Playfair, aged twenty-six, became a victim of the Handley Page Hampden's tendency to oversteer in a rapid turn to port when he lost control doing just that while flying solo near his Doncaster base and died in the crash. Number 7 was then a training squadron, in effect an OTU (Operational Training Unit), recently re-equipped with Hampdens for that purpose, having had Whitleys for the

All the pilots on the early operations were regulars from before the war. Here, posing with a Heyford in 1938, are three who went on the 4 September Brunsbüttel raid. P/O Grant sits third from right, P/O Bob Turner standing centre Sgt Charles Bowen stands sixth from right. Bowen was killed with all his crew in the Norway campaign, 12 April 1940.

Wellingtons of 9 Squadron with their pre-war letters KA feature in this advertisement for Vickers-Armstrongs, August 1939. L4275 KA-H, top of picture middle right, was shot down at Brunsbüttel, 4 September 1939, in the first air battle of the war.

previous year. After being disbanded and reformed, No. 7 would be the first RAF squadron to fly four-engined bombers (Short Stirlings).

So sensational was the news about Brunsbüttel that King George VI wanted to hear the story for himself and Squadron Leader Lamb was sent by royal command to Buckingham Palace on 8 September, the date of the next Bomber Command fatality, and it was 9 Squadron again, recorded thus:

> 'During air firing practice at Berners Heath an accident occurred to aircraft L4320. The following lost their lives: Pilot Officer Rosofsky, P/O Clifford-Jones, AC1 McGreery, AC1 Purdie.'

Also killed but not mentioned in the ORB was twenty-year-old Aircraftman Second Class William Hilsdon, on secondment from training squadron No. 215. And it was McGreevy, not McGreery. The accident seems to have been a case of pilot error with the aircraft flying into trees and crashing near Thetford.

The second pilot, Pilot Officer Bruce Innes Clifford-Jones, age twenty-two, was from New Plymouth, Taranaki – the second New Zealander to die in the Second World War. The first, Pilot Officer Cedric Whittington, had been killed the day before in a Coastal Command Hudson of 224 Squadron. No. 9 Squadron was soon to lose two more of its Kiwi officers.

A few minutes before midnight on this day, 8 September, Whitleys of 77 and 102 Squadrons set off from Driffield aiming for the Ruhr on a leaflet raid. The plan was to fly to the Jutland Peninsula, turn south, drop the leaflets, turn west and come home. Some of them did that. One of the flight commanders of 102, Squadron Leader Murray, got so completely lost that, after dropping their leaflets, the crew saw city lights and assumed it was Paris when in fact it was Berlin. Taking a course for Driffield from 'Paris', they seemed to take a very long time to find the French coast and ran out of petrol. Force-landing in a field, they greeted the French soldiers with cheers, only to find that they were Germans and the field was near Itzehoe, roughly halfway between Hamburg and Brunsbüttel. Murray and his crew, uninjured, became the first complete team to be taken prisoner.

Coming home in poor visibility, a Canadian pilot, Flying Officer Gordon Raphael of No. 77 was way off track and decided to land at the first opportunity, which came at an aerodrome south-west of Paris, by the village of Buc. Taxying in the fog he ran into a parked aeroplane, a single-engined Dewoitine fighter, and wrote off both. No one was hurt. He would have an even more exciting time in a Whitley on the night of 18/19 May 1940 (*see Chapter Six*).

Also off track was Flying Officer Cogman in his 102 Squadron Whitley, flying over neutral Belgium with, it is said, another 102 Whitley behind. Fairey Firefly II and Fairey Fox VI aircraft, of the Belgian air force, intercepted. The Firefly II was an open-cockpit, single-seater biplane, first flying in 1929, while the Fox VI was a reconnaissance version of the 1926 two-seater light bomber. Both machines were favoured by the Belgians if by few others.

Cogman was forced to land while the rear gunner in the other Whitley shot down one of the Foxes, with the crew baling out and landing little worse for the experience. Cogman and crew were interned and later sent home. Protests by the Belgian authorities were met with apologies and, according to one source, the offer of a new aircraft of more recent origin to replace the lost Fox, which was politely refused.

CHAPTER 3

How bad can it get?

The first week of the war had been a shambles for the RAF, characterised by bloody disasters at Brunsbüttel and Wilhelmshaven, fatal crashes in training, and crews getting lost in the dark. The rest of the month was much, much worse.

A Wellington of 75 Squadron took off from Harwell, Oxfordshire, on a training flight at 20.00 on 18 September. At 06.40 the next morning, with no petrol left and no idea where they were, the crew abandoned ship and parachuted into north Glamorgan, not far from Aberdare, about 100 miles from home.

Within a few hours of that, a Whitley of 51 Squadron took off with its elevators still locked, stalled, and crashed, killing pilot and second pilot; a Wellington of 99 Squadron collided on take-off with another aircraft, injuring all crew, of whom one died the following day; a Battle of 207 Squadron flew into a Gloucestershire hillside in a rainstorm with two men killed; and a Blenheim of 82 Squadron had both engines fail and crashed with no-one hurt. That was all on 19 September. On 20 September the losses were not accidental.

No. 88 Squadron, RAF Bomber Command, had left Boscombe Down, Wiltshire, for France and Mourmelon-le-Grand, near Reims, and made ready with sixteen Fairey Battles – part of that optimistically named Advanced Air Striking Force, of Battles, Bristol Blenheims and Hawker Hurricanes, under the command of Air Vice Marshal Playfair. In range of the enemy, based on foreign territory, their job was hazily defined and politically sensitive.

Mourmelon was an historic airfield, one of the earliest, in the midst of the First World War battlegrounds of the Marne and the Ardenne and the site of some notable aeronautical pioneering. Henry Farman took off there for his distance record of 234.2 kilometres (145.5 miles) on 3 November 1909 in a Farman Brothers aircraft – an astonishing improvement of 100 kilometres on the previous best set only three months before by Louis Paulhan in a Voisin. Édouard Nieuport set his world speed record there on 21 June 1911, flying 133 kilometres (82.7 miles) in one hour in a machine of his own making.

The machines flown by 88 Squadron would soon be setting some records of a very different sort. When first built the Battle far outperformed its predecessors, the Hawker Hart, Hind and Audax biplanes, and was faster than any known fighter. By September 1939, several new and different aircraft were known about, such as the Me109 and the Ju88. The handsome, elegant Battle had been overtaken. Now it was relatively slow, and disastrously under-armed for daylight flying.

In the strange, tense quiet of the 'Phoney War', for the AASF there was only reconnaissance, with or without the permission and escort of their French allies, but these trips could easily expose the Battle. At Mourmelon one of the armourers was a Belfast boy and a regular from 1936, Sergeant John Henry Maguire known as Mick:

> 'The Battle wasn't much use against fighters. There are quite a few crews of three buried in the local churchyards around there.'

Reconnaissance meant flights into Germany – not too far, perhaps thirty miles – trying to spot any build-up of forces. On this day, 20 September, three of 88 Squadron's Battles were some way north of Mourmelon at the point where the Belgian, Dutch and German borders meet, near Aachen (Aix-la-Chapelle to the French and the Belgians). According to French reports, between 1,500 and 1,800 German bombers were stationed in that region. Actual figures, according to *The Luftwaffe War Diaries*, were 336 single-engined fighters, 180 twin-engined fighters, and 280 bombers. The attention of the German air force, for the moment, was on bombing Poland. Fighters stationed on the Western Front were there simply to defend German airspace and prevent Allied spying.

The three of 88 Squadron were attacked by three Me109s of JG2. Two Messerschmitts went for Battle K9245 and shot it down in flames, killing pilot Flight Sergeant Douglas Page, observer Sergeant Alfred

Eggington, and w/opAG Aircraftman First Class Edward Radford, all pre-war regulars, obviously, and with an average age of twenty-five.

Also going down in French territory but with the pilot Flying Officer Reg Graveley managing a crash landing, was Battle K9242. Observer Sergeant William Everett later died of his wounds and w/opAG Aircraftman First Class David John was killed outright. Graveley was awarded the Empire Gallantry Medal (later renamed as the George Cross) for pulling Everett and the body of John out of the burning aircraft, suffering severe burns himself.

In the third Battle, K9243, the observer – Sergeant Letchford – was manning the gun and shot down one of the Messerschmitts. French pilots in their Curtiss Hawks had already shot down at least two Me109s but this was the first RAF success of the war. Frederick Arthur Letchford, promoted to Pilot Officer, would be killed in a Blenheim of 88 Squadron over The Netherlands on 28 August 1941.

News of the Western Front at this time rather depended on communiqués from the French government in Paris. The activity on 20 September merited the following, from Communiqué 37:

> 'During air operations on Wednesday, a German fighter aircraft was shot down by British aircraft in France.'

Just how curious the war was at this stage is shown by a report in the British press of patents filed in London by German firms. The Patent Office was the only place where, for example, Junkers could protect its novel system of using exhaust gases to assist in the propulsion of the aircraft. Four more German patents variously concerned the use of powdered fuels in aero engines. Technical spies were hardly needed when there was the Patent Office to publish the latest information.

The maximum retail price of butter was fixed at 1s 7d a pound (8p); the equivalent would be about £2 for the modern 250 gram pack. The price of granulated sugar was fixed at 3½d a pound. Marshall and Snelgrove offered a coat in finest quality Canadian skunk at 79 guineas (about £4,000 modern equivalent), while Liberty had a pure wool, youthful frock with Tyrolean silk scarf in a number of colours at five guineas (£250). Austin Reed was selling good quality camel coats for men at nine guineas. Petrol rationing meant fewer buses, so the number of standing passengers allowed was increased to a maximum of eight.

Out in the country, farmers were being offered a £2 an acre incentive to plough up grassland for arable crops and were advised to concentrate on producing bigger, fatter pigs rather than the lean baconers of latter days. Billingsgate market reopened but supplies were unpredictable; Dover soles fetched 2s a pound, lobsters 2s, whole cod ninepence ha'penny.

Over in France, the boys of 88 Squadron had a lecture from the CO on the Maginot Line and one of the audience pointed out a rather large gap in it called Belgium. What was to stop the Germans coming through there, he wanted to know. A few squadrons of Fairey Battles?

On the UK mainland in 1939 there was still uncertainty about how, when or if to deploy the squadrons of Bomber Command. Some had no work for weeks on end. Guy Gibson and 83 Squadron had moved to Ringway, Manchester, to avoid possible destruction on the ground by German bombers:

> 'Each day all we had to do was to test our aeroplanes. This usually took about half an hour and involved some pretty good beat-ups of the clubhouse. The rest of the day we spent having baths and shaving and making ourselves generally presentable until the bus took us to the pub at five o'clock.'

Otherwise, in the rest of Bomber Command there was training, night-time nickelling, reconnaissance, and the occasional daylight raid on the German navy. A typical example of the latter came on 26 September when 144 Squadron, flying Hampdens from Hemswell, Lincolnshire, on their first op of the war, was ordered to send twelve machines to find enemy ships reported in the North Sea. They saw nothing apart from a couple of submarines, unidentified, and came home.

In another part of the same sea, near the Fisher Bank, the same policy in reverse was being carried out. Luftwaffe scouts reported seeing the whole of the British Home Fleet steaming along. There were two battleships, two battle-cruisers, an aircraft carrier, seven cruisers and six destroyers. The Germans, seemingly as optimistic as the British, sent nine Heinkel 111s and four Junkers 88s. One pilot claimed a possible hit, soon translated by wishful thinking and the propaganda machine into the sinking of the *Ark Royal*, which, along with all the other ships, suffered no damage whatsoever.

Three Battles of 103 Squadron, based at Challerange, near Verdun, set out on 27 September for the Rhine, flying fairly low. Three Curtiss Hawks of the French air force, mistaking them for Germans, fell on them. The American Hawk was a single-seat fighter, the contemporary and equivalent of the British Hurricane and the German Me109, and certainly superior to the Battle. Disaster was averted when the section leader, Flying Officer Wells, fired off the colours of the day and took his formation down to tree-top height.

The French, recognising their friends at last, flew away. Had they stayed a little longer they might have had some enemies to engage, as they were replaced in the morning sky by three Me109s of JG52. The pilot of one Messerschmitt, Joseph Scherm, engaged Battle K9271, pilot Flying Officer Vipan and, in an exchange of fire with the single Vickers machine gun operated by the observer Sergeant Vickers, was himself killed while severely wounding Vickers and damaging the Battle's engine.

Vipan came down in a field, just on the French side of the Maginot Line and had the help of a French soldier in pulling Vickers out. A column of smoke rising near by was, said the soldier, the Messerschmitt that he had seen being brought down. Sergeant John Henry Vickers, married to Peggy, from Withernsea in the East Riding, died of his wounds, having been awarded the Medaille Militaire.

Arthur Lushington Vipan would have more close shaves before being transferred to Training Command. In 1944, as a thirty-year-old Squadron Leader he would begin retraining as a heavy bomber pilot. On the point of moving up to four engines, he and his crew would be killed when his Wellington exploded in mid-air over Buckinghamshire, night of 16 October.

No. 110, the squadron of Doran DFC, who had lost Flying Officer Emden and crew on day two of the war, was ordered to mount reconnaissance missions from Wattisham, Suffolk, to the Münster/Osnabrück region on 27 September. Their Blenheims took off early, around 7.30am.

Acting Wing Commander Ivan Cameron, the squadron CO and leading the operation, was shot down many miles from his destination,

The Bristol Blenheim played a huge part in the early months of the war, and many brave men were lost on missions that exposed its weaknesses, trying to fulfil tasks for which the aircraft was unfit.

near Kiel, believed to have been the victim of Feldwebel Klaus Faber of JG1, with all three crew killed. Cameron was a long-serving officer, having joined the RAF in 1927 and was probably the first Australian airman to be killed in action in this war.

Another 110 Blenheim, skippered by Flying Officer Donald Strachan, was lost without trace but German records have it as shot down into the Heligoland Bight by Leutnant Helmut Henz of JG77. At this time, the Bight was the route into and out of northern Germany, avoiding neutral countries, but quite what Wing Commander Cameron was doing so far north at Kiel, we cannot know.

The second op for 144 Squadron started out in similar fashion to their first. It was 29 September and ships of the German navy were reported in the Heligoland Bight, where they often were. Twelve Hampdens in two sections, led by Wing Commander James Cunningham, the squadron's CO and a married man of thirty-one, and his number two, Squadron Leader Lindley, took off in the late afternoon. One of Cunningham's flight had to return while the rest searched and again found nothing.

Lindley's flight discovered two destroyers and went in – or tried to. German navy flak was very competently handled and three aircraft could not get within bombing distance, while the others did bomb but could not stay to see what happened. They came home and waited for Cunningham.

Still looking, the CO's five approached the East Friesian islands from the north. In sight of Wangerooge, the first in the chain, a considerable force of Me109s swooped on them and, after a brief battle, shot down every one. Four men were rescued by the Germans, the rest all died, including Cunningham.

The Air Ministry promptly issued a statement, reported in the papers the next day:

> 'Units of the Royal Air Force to-day carried out attacks on ships of the German fleet in the Heligoland Bight. In spite of formidable anti-aircraft fire the attacks were pressed home at low altitude. Some of our aircraft have not yet returned.'

The German news agency also commented on the same incident, saying that six British aeroplanes attacked German warships near

Heligoland without success. Afterwards, German fighter aircraft engaged the British machines as they were returning home and shot down five.

In a separate announcement, the Admiralty once more stated that no British warship has been sunk or hit by any aerial attack.

Despite all this evidence, both sides continued to believe, or hope, that somebody someday would find a naval vessel on purpose and sink it, thus altering the course of the war. Next day, another aerial policy, armed reconnaissance over Germany from French bases by Fairey Battles, had its most severe test yet. Unusually, there was a full and dramatic account in the press, courtesy of the Ministry of Information.

Five Battles of 150 Squadron, based at Ecury-sur-Coole, were sent to reconnoitre 'a particular position' on 30 September, near Saarbrücken, behind the Siegfried Line, where strong defences could be expected. After successfully negotiating the flak, the Battle crews saw nine Messerschmitt 109s coming at them from above, in front, a true case of bandits twelve o'clock high. Another six 109s came in from the starboard side. The tactic was for groups of fighters to take on one Battle at a time:

> 'Their method was to wheel, dive, and come in under the tail of our aircraft. Intense fighting lasted for 35 minutes. Three of our machines were shot down and another made a forced landing, but of the twelve men forming the crews, eight were seen to escape by parachute.'

Pilot Officer John Saunders's aircraft was probably the first victim, as it fell not far from Saarbrücken. The navigator Sergeant Springett got out and was taken prisoner; the pilot, aged twenty, and w/opAG Aircraftman First Class Donald Thomas, aged nineteen, were killed. All the other machines made the short distance across the border before going down. Flight Lieutenant Hyde-Parker, pilot, and the wounded w/opAG Aircraftman First Class Jones jumped at Metzing, in Moselle, but navigator Sergeant William Cole did not survive. Navigator Sergeant Webber was injured when he jumped but his aircraft crashed and killed his captain Flying Officer Fernald Corelli and w/opAG, nineteen-year-old AC1 Kenneth Gay.

The fourth Battle was abandoned by its crew, all parachuting to safety so, if Sergeant Cole did jump, that was indeed eight:

> 'The squadron leader's machine (Sq/Ldr W. M. L. Macdonald) alone was left but he flew on to finish the job. In the tail of the aircraft, the air-gunner kept up a steady fire. A stream of bullets hit the leading Messerschmitt. The enemy machine swerved and in a second burst into flames and plunged to earth. Keeping up his fire the gunner landed further bursts into the second fighter. With smoke pouring from the nose it went down in a spin. Shaken by the gunner's steady and accurate fire, the 13 remaining Germans gave up the fight.'

Yes, well, Macdonald would have been very foolish indeed if he had flown on to finish the job. In his run back towards France, two 109s were claimed by Aircraftman First Class Murcar and the Germans admitted the loss. Giving up the fight was not as likely as running out of petrol and not wanting to go too far into France.

The navigator, Sergeant F. H. Gardiner, was wounded in the head and the aircraft was full of holes pouring petrol everywhere, but the pilot stopped one of the leaks with his handkerchief. They got home somehow only to find the undercarriage would not lower properly as they tried to glide in with a stopped engine, out of fuel.

The landing was a spectacular disaster, with the aircraft's undercart digging in to the grass, causing a cartwheel and a sudden bursting into flames. Pilot and navigator were thrown clear; the gunner was trapped. The navigator pulled him out, smothering his burning clothes with his hands.

Alexander Murcar was awarded the Distinguished Flying Medal, the first of the war, transferred to Coastal Command and was lost in a Hudson aircraft of 224 Squadron on 15 April 1940. William MacDonald had the officers' version, the Distinguished Flying Cross, and would later become Air Chief Marshal Sir William. Sergeant Gardiner received the British Empire Medal for saving his fellow crewman from the fire.

Daylight reconnaissance over Germany was removed from duty for the Battle squadrons although not, as we shall see, for the Blenheims.

> 'Gunnery superiority lies overwhelmingly with the fighter. The bomber's guns, to put it bluntly, are there to give the bomber's crew a cheerful feeling that they are hitting back. They are "hurrah" equipment. For bringing down fighters they cannot be looked on as enormously effective.'
>
>   *Aeronautics* magazine, October 1939.

> 'A device is now being fitted as standard to RAF aircraft which automatically prevents fire breaking out both in the air and on the ground. The device is known as the Graviner and is the invention of Captain H. M. Salmond, a retired naval officer. It consists of a copper bottle which contains methyl bromide under pressure, and an arrangement of distribution piping. When activated, the methyl bromide instantly evaporates, produces an intense cooling effect, and dense extinguishing fumes are evolved.'
>
>   *Aeronautics* magazine, October 1939.

One day in late September there was consternation in the crew room when a Morse message came through to Ringway from Scampton on the private wireless set that 83 Squadron had rigged up to avoid the usual hours of delay when booking long-distance telephone calls. Guy Gibson was there as it was decoded:

> ' "From Base to 83rd detachment, Ringway." We waited. We were going to France? We were going to Iceland? This was war. This was the real thing. "Return Base P.M. for concentrated night-flying training." There were yells of disappointment. "Night flying, what a bind." "Leaflets. O Christ." (When we got to Scampton) Night flying training had been cancelled. Why, we didn't know. We were now standing by for shipping strikes. Every day they wanted nine aircraft from each squadron bombed up, ready to start at half an hour's notice. And so the days dragged on.'

While the men of No. 83 were kicking their heels waiting for ships to be spotted, the senior commanders seemingly drew straws and tossed coins to see how the war might be waged next.

Sending Whitleys to Berlin was asking a great deal of the crew and the aircraft. That long journey was the very limit of its endurance, as was proved on the night of 1/2 October, when four Whitleys of 10 Squadron were given that target, the first time such a thing had been attempted. The weather was terrible and the Whitleys flew as high as possible to get above it, meaning the crews were relying on oxygen, were suffering dreadfully from the cold with a grossly inadequate heating system, and the pilot had increased problems in flying the machine, which did not handle well at, say, 18,000 feet although its service ceiling was supposed to be much higher.

Three crews claimed to have reached Berlin and dropped their loaflets there. One had an oxygen failure forcing the pilot down to 9,000 feet to revive two crew members who had collapsed. This alerted the anti-aircraft gunners, so that was another first for the night – being fired at by the Berlin guns that were supposed to make that city impregnable from the air.

The fourth crew, led by Australian Flight Lieutenant John Allsop, sent a message to say that Berlin had not been found and that the nickels had been dropped elsewhere (over what was probably Denmark). This aircraft had been in the air for ten minutes short of seven hours when the Scottish wireless operator, Aircraftman First Class John Bell, transmitted another message, asking for a fix.

There were three categories of fix. A first class fix was obtained when three ground stations on the UK mainland bounced a radio signal off the aircraft and, receiving a strong signal back, found their intersecting point. The position was calculated, probably within a mile, and transmitted to the aircraft. Lesser degrees of confidence, due to weakness of signal or fewer ground stations receiving, produced second and third class fixes. As bad weather interfered with the process, poorer quality fixes had to be given when precision was most needed.

Home for Allsop and crew was Dishforth, in the North Riding; the fix placed the aircraft about 180 miles east of the Berwickshire coast, roughly halfway between Denmark and Scotland.

They were never heard of again. In such cases, in those days, crews of their own squadron and possibly others would rush to take off and search the sea for hours on end. Very occasionally they found their men in a dinghy. Sometimes they found just the dinghy. More often, they found nothing at all.

If the three objectives of nickelling were, in order of importance, training through experience, reconnaissance, and propaganda, then the raid as a whole might have been called a success.

There were no more losses in action for a while, although training was still proving dangerous. Crashes on take-off and landing were the most common, an exception being a Blenheim of 108 Squadron, captained by a Londoner, Sergeant Phillip Hemsley, which took off without alarm from Bicester, headed for the Isle of Man and disappeared completely.

In France, Blenheims of 57 and 114 Squadrons were sent over the German border on 13 October. The objective was to discover whether troops were being moved from Poland to the Western Front. The Blenheims would try to observe traffic on the railways and autobahns in deepest Germany, fly back to England to refuel and deliver their intelligence, than back to France to do it again. The CO of 57 Squadron, based at Metz, Wing Commander H. M. A. Day was ordered to reconnoitre the rail and road links between Hamm and Hannover. They didn't get very far into enemy territory before the fighters found them and shot them down near Birkenfeld, south of Bernkastel.

Flying Officer Norman set off for the Münster/Bremen area, did his work and returned towards his base in England, but bad weather forced him down near Harpenden. No one was hurt, while Pilot Officer Thompson of 114 Squadron based at Villeneuve-les-Vertus, on a similar mission, encountered flak and fighters together and fell to earth. Alexander Lumsden, the w/opAG, was twenty-one; observer George Marwood was twenty-five. Pilot and captain Kenneth Thompson was nineteen years old.

From time to time, Whitleys of 77 Squadron were temporarily relocated to Villeneuve and from there on 15 October four took off for a nickelling raid on Frankfurt. They were recalled but one did not acknowledge the signal and so presumably did not receive it. A signal transmitted from the aircraft led to the belief that it was heading for home base at Driffield, but nothing further was heard. The Germans reported shooting it down by anti-aircraft fire near Darmstadt, about twenty miles short of Frankfurt. All the crew survived the crash and were taken prisoner except the pilot, Flight Lieutenant Roland Williams, whose body was found outside the aircraft. He had been killed and thrown clear while saving the rest.

Next morning the Blenheims of 57 Squadron were reconnoitring again, this time in the Wesel-Bocholt area, just north of the Rhine, not so far into Germany for the work but still with a great deal of it to fly over if they were to return home to England. Following the river Ems northwards to the sea, Blenheim Mark 1, captained by Flying Officer Michael James Casey, was found by Leutnant Hans Rosenboom near Lingen. The crew survived to become POWs. Casey, the only officer, would be sent to Stalag Luft III and, after the Great Escape, be one of the fifty murdered.

More Whitleys, more nickelling, more losses – this was the action towards the end of the month of October. While the usual crashes were happening to all types of aircraft in training, 77 Squadron lost another Whitley, somewhere in the sea with no bodies or wreckage found, and 51 Squadron lost three crash landing in France, heavily iced up on returning from Germany, with no fatalities. One of those three was abandoned but the tail gunner didn't hear the order to jump. Sergeant Griffin was still in his turret when the aircraft came down but had nothing more than a few bruises to show his mates in the mess afterwards.

Arriving at 9 Squadron, Honington, from 38 Squadron to take up one of the captain's positions in A Flight under Squadron Leader Lamb, made vacant after Brunsbüttel, was Frank Cyril Petts. He would finish the war as Flight Lieutenant DFC and Bar. In 1939 he was a sergeant pilot, but no ordinary one.

At 38 Squadron, Petts had worked with an august body called the Air Fighting Development Establishment and various techniques had been prescribed for dealing with fighter attacks. Petts:

> 'The official theory at that time was that fighters had such a small speed advantage over the modern bomber that any attack must become a stern chase and, since we mostly flew in sections of three in a Vic, of course the fighters would do likewise.'

In a stern chase, a straightforward battle would develop between the fixed guns of the fighter, whose pilot had to fly along his own line of fire, and the more flexible options of the bombers' moveable, aimable guns in hydraulic turrets. Should evasive action become necessary – bearing in mind the absolute necessity for the bombers to stick together – one technique was 'Rotate', in which the two wing-men of the section orbited the leader, clockwise or anticlockwise, depending. Another was 'Scissors', which began like 'Rotate' but fooled the attackers by reversing at halfway to original positions. The leader, neither scissoring nor rotating, would have to fend for himself. Not content with the orthodox, Squadron Leader Lamb devised his own defensive manoeuvre which didn't have a name except when it was being discussed out of Lamb's hearing. Petts:

> 'The other sections wouldn't touch it but we had to, and we tried it first on 27 October 1939 with Spitfires from 66 Squadron pretending to be Germans. As they turned to attack, we changed from Vic to a vertical step formation, with me at the bottom. The Spits closed in. Our leader ordered a sudden throttling back, which can be sound practice for upsetting a fighter pilot but not in a close formation of Wellingtons stepped down vertically.'

The reason it was a bad idea was that pilots B and C could not be sure of throttling back at exactly the same time and by exactly the same amount as pilot A.

The pilot in the number two aircraft, Flying Officer John Chandler, the other Brunsbüttel replacement, found himself in Lamb's slipstream and could not stop his aircraft going into a sudden descent. Petts, at number three below, saw him coming and threw his Wellington into such a steep dive that the man in his rear turret, Sergeant Robertson, knocked himself out on the roof of it.

To illustrate the somewhat makeshift nature of bomber crews at that time, Robertson flew mainly as the observer/navigator, manning the rear turret when required. Operating the beam guns, which fired through apertures in the fuselage side, and the under-gun in the dustbin turret, was the wireless operator. Petts had a full-time front gunner, and a second pilot who deputised as bomb aimer. Squadron Leader Lamb had the same crew make-up of five altogether. Chandler had his second pilot but then only two young AC2s, one eighteen years old and training as a wireless operator, the other aged nineteen, normally ground crew. Petts:

> 'Our number two, above me, dropped like a stone. I reacted by putting the nose down on full throttle, which bounced

Sergeant Robertson around in his turret and KO'd him, and shot Aircraftman Kemp right out of his dustbin turret into the fuselage.'

According to Squadron Leader Lamb, there was nothing wrong with his idea. They just weren't doing it properly so they had to try again three days later. Petts's attention was frantically divided, between his air speed indicator and the aircraft above:

'We were at 800 feet, just below the cloud base and, as before, changed from Vic to vertical step and throttled sharply back.'

Chandler, from being behind Lamb, was suddenly in front. Petts:

'I looked up and saw Chandler hit Lamb's starboard wing with his tailfin, just behind the engine.'

This brought Chandler's nose up and a smash was inevitable. Petts stuck his own nose hard down and didn't pull out until he was level with the tree tops. Robertson's voice came on the intercom: 'They've missed us'. He'd seen the two bombers fall past his turret, locked together, breaking up as they spun to oblivion. Petts:

'A group of us were in the sergeants' mess later, talking about what had happened. I took a draw on my very large brandy when I realised that Lamb's rear gunner, Sgt Smith, who was actually an observer like Robertson and had been with Lamb at Brunsbüttel, was sitting next to me. This I thought pretty odd as I'd seen him getting into the aircraft. "How on earth did you get out of that?" I said. Smith replied that he'd been in his turret when F/O Torkington-Leech, second pilot as gunner, famous as the first man to claim to have shot a German down, had said that he would occupy the turret in question, so Smith came back to the mess in a huff.'

In the scramble to find and train aircrew, more were being lost in accidents than on ops (the numbers for 1939 were seventy-eight aircraft on training flights, sixty-eight on operations). Squadron Leader

Lamb, New Zealander, regal interviewee and one of the first notable flyers in these hostilities, and all his crew were dead, including Torkington-Leech and two more veterans of Brunsbüttel, Sergeant Cyril Bryant and Leading Aircraftman Stanley Hawkins. John Chandler and his three crew were dead too. His second pilot, Colin Cameron, another Kiwi, was on loan from 215 training squadron.

All the families were offered funerals with full air force honours at All Saints Church, Honington. Some chose that; some preferred their own home churchyard.

The wreckage lay for weeks by the Rectory at Sapiston. While two other squadrons had crashed a Wellington each with only one aircrew death, 9 Squadron had now lost five of these aircraft with twenty-four dead.

The reconnaissance Blenheims were busy on this day too. A pair of them fell to Luftwaffe ace Werner Mölders, veteran of the Spanish Civil War in which he shot down fourteen government aircraft. He'd already opened his account in this war with a French Curtiss Hawk, been made commanding officer of III.Gruppe/JG53 at Weisbaden-Erbenheim, and would go on to a century of victories before being compulsorily retired at age twenty-eight and dying as a passenger in an air crash.

The two Blenheims were from 18 Squadron, based at Méharicourt, Picardy, and were the squadron's first losses after being operational for two weeks. Flight Lieutenant Alan Dilnot had hardly got into Germany before Mölders found him and shot him down near Malborn, in the Bernkastel district of the Rhineland, and Flying Officer Dennis Elliot didn't manage much further – Wehlen. The crash sites were so close together that Mölders in his Me109 must have discovered the Blenheims flying together and shot them down in turn, killing all crew.

Things were no better at the other end of Germany where another reconnaissance Blenheim, flown by Australian Pilot Officer William McCracken of 139 Squadron, had come in from Wyton and fallen at Haselünne, not very far from Lingen where Michael Casey was taken.

Over the next week, Hampdens, Ansons, Blenheims, Battles, Wellingtons and Whitleys were lost, crashed or otherwise written off in training, with nineteen men killed, plus two more recce Blenheims of 57 Squadron. The returns on these missions were, as it turned out, entirely negative apart from a superbly detailed photographic map of

L4260 was one of the first of the Wellington Mark I to be delivered to the RAF in January 1939. It never flew an op, being transferred to training duties in the October.

Barnes Wallis's geodetic construction can clearly be seen on the inside of this Wellington, along with the amount of consideration given to crew comfort.

the Seigfried Line. 'A Wing Commander', looking back from 1943 in his book *Bombers' Battle* gave his opinion thus:

> 'Much of this work (by the Blenheims) and the information so gained went for nothing, because the people most concerned, the Dutch and the Belgians, and to some extent the French, made no use of it in preparing effective resistance to the German advance (in May 1940).'

While some squadrons still had nothing to do – such as Guy Gibson's 83 – and had to keep themselves busy with bombing competitions and suchlike, other squadrons did armed reconnaissances, which were sweep searches for hostile ships in the North Sea. If they saw anything at all, it was most likely a couple of fishing vessels off Yarmouth. From this time until the ban was lifted against bombing enemy territory, these sweeps would go on and on, each one usually about five hours, searching the grey ocean and almost always finding nothing.

Finding nothing was probably fortunate for these crews, although not viewed so at the time. If they had found a warship, the rule was still to go in low. 'A Wing Commander' again:

> '... it was of no use to attack a warship from a very low level; a bomb dropped from under 1,000 feet travels too slow to have much chance of penetrating an armoured deck.'

And, as already discovered, if they didn't penetrate they usually bounced off. There was also a misapprehension about German warships' armoury. Guy Gibson:

> 'One squadron of twelve aircraft was sent to attack three destroyers off Heligoland. Only six came back and they had the queerest story to tell. They found that a destroyer does not possess machine guns, as they had been told, but very strong AA fire in the shape of light flak guns which makes a single low level attack practically suicidal unless backed up by waves of aircraft.'

(Gibson was writing about the events of 14 December and 99 Squadron, of which more later.)

'A Wing Commander':

> 'There could be no question of attacking a warship without expecting heavy casualties.'

True, except that nobody was expecting it then. Gibson:

> 'We were lucky – we weren't the guinea pigs but (other squadrons) had to pay the price. We did not know a thing about aerial warfare and it was up to us to learn.'

Everyone knew that the 'no civilians' stricture could not last and that both sides could be sure of being bombed at home eventually. In turn, the bombers would be allowed to do the job for which they were designed, but it wasn't only Guy Gibson who realised that nothing was known about how best to set about the work.

All right. Let us imagine that we have orders to bomb an important industrial target in a well-defended area of Germany. The view at the time was that four bombers to a target would be enough, but suppose we really wanted to make sure and hammer it. Suppose it was a big target, like the Krupp works at Essen, and we wanted to send a decent sort of force to it, say, twenty-four Wellingtons. What will be the briefing? Here's your target for tonight, chaps, off you go? Except it wasn't tonight. It was today. Wellingtons were day bombers.

Nobody had ever sent that many bombers to one land target so, while several squadrons were sea sweeping, more Blenheims were being lost on recce flights, Whitleys went nickelling and aircraft of every type were being written off in training, plans were drawn up to see how co-ordinated bombing might be done in a modern air raid.

Six Wellingtons each from Nos 9, 37, 38 and 115 Squadrons took off after breakfast on 28 November, and rendezvoused over Upper Heyford. Under the direction of Wing Commander R. A. A. Cole of No. 9, they formed up in five minutes and set off for Rhyl, north Wales. The weather was unkind and the formation had to drop at times from 6,000 feet to 2,000 in rain and cloud over the Welsh hills. But they stayed together and arrived at Rhyll to find cloud down to 2,000 feet, when the idea was to deliver a high-level attack, defined as 10,000 feet, on targets of opportunity. The Wingco decided to stay up top and try to find targets through gaps in the cloud, while the specially assembled defences of Rhyl fired blanks at them.

Here is the Wing Commander's report:

'The exercise was most useful and many points of instructional value were learned:

1. A force of 24 aircraft could put in a co-ordinated attack. First squadron to attack: 9 Squadron. Time over target 12.00 hours. Last squadron to attack: 115 Squadron. Time over target 12.15 hours. This time could be reduced under more favourable weather conditions.'

On the night of 17/18 August 1943, three precision targets at Peenemünde would be bombed by 600 four-engined aircraft in three waves of 200, and each wave would bomb in ten minutes. In November 1939, three months into the war, this exercise set out to prove that two dozen Wellingtons could attack a target in daylight in a quarter of an hour. When orders were eventually given for the first night raids on Germany, four bombing hours would be allowed for 100 aircraft.

2. 'Rendezvous of squadrons can be carried out successfully provided care is taken in co-ordination prior to exercise and if squadrons are not rushed.'

Memo to Air Officers Commanding, Royal Air Force, World War Two: do not ask your squadrons to rush.

3. 'Get away. It will appear at the moment that we shall have to accept the fact that a Wing is unable to form up again quickly after an attack. Flights of six will have to keep together for support after the attack. On completion of attack, No. 9 Squadron turned quickly off target and when clear of A-A fire reduced to 140mph and continued for 30 minutes at that speed but still remaining squadrons did not close up.'

In a little over two weeks, German fighters would be closing up and demonstrating what they could do to flights of six Wellingtons trying to keep together for support in daylight.

4. 'The most difficult aspect of the whole exercise under trying weather conditions was the selecting of a target and passing the order to attack it to the Wing. Unless good weather conditions prevail one is on top of the target before any definite action can be taken, so the passing of an order selecting the target becomes a nearly impossible task.'

So, a choice would have to be made, between bombing on clear, sunny days only or selecting the target in advance.

5. 'It is considered essential that good field or sea glasses should be provided for this type of commitment. No. 37 flew in pairs and the other squadrons in "Vic". It is considered that one type of formation should be adopted.'

This was the state of the art of bombing in Britain. Crews of skill and limitless courage would fly in pairs or a V and look for their targets with binoculars.

It would be a while before the many points of instructional value could be put into practice in land raids but the German navy was still on the list and there was considerable pressure on the RAF from – for example – Winston Churchill, First Lord of the Admiralty, to score a major hit on the enemy by sinking a capital ship.

There were many reconnaissance flights looking for suitable targets. The word 'reconnaissance' makes these missions seem somehow easier than bombing, but recce planes had to get in close and the danger was the same as in an armed attack. *The Times* of Monday 27 November:

'Important naval bases in North-West Germany, including Heligoland, were visited (25 November) by aircraft of the Royal Air Force. Bad weather, with snow, ice and heavy rain, and the failing light of the late afternoon, made the task particularly difficult and hazardous.

'One pilot, flying low, was able to take the defence momentarily by surprise. He was above the naval base with his camera in action before the ground batteries could open fire, but within a few seconds of his arrival he was subjected

to an intense barrage of "flaming onions" and pom-pom
shells which burst in groups of red, black and orange smoke,
and the pilot had to resort to violent evasive action to escape.'

Flaming onions were a kind of fiery flare, fired in volleys from a
38mm revolving-barrel gun that was designed in the late nineteenth
century as normal artillery but brought into use against aircraft in the
First World War. The flare shells were especially dangerous for those
machines that were fabric covered. The name came from the flares'
appearance of being connected in a string, in the way that onions
were sold in those days.

Also on 27 November Prime Minister Chamberlain was saying that
'Our wider objective is to bring into being a new Europe, animated
by a spirit of freedom, good will, mutual tolerance, and co-operation
between nations.'

Our narrower objective remained the sinking of warships. Air
Ministry statement, issued late on 3 December:

> 'A strong formation of Royal Air Force bombers to-day
> carried out an attack on German warships in the vicinity of
> Heligoland. Direct hits were obtained with heavy bombs. A
> considerable anti-aircraft fire was met, and a Messerschmitt
> fighter, the only enemy fighter encountered, was shot down.
> All our aircraft have returned.'

The formation was twenty-four Wellingtons of 38 and 149 Squadrons.
They were out looking on spec, as it were, for ships, and to photograph
Heligoland and anything else of interest. Heligoland is actually two
islands with straits between, and that's where two cruisers were found
to be loitering. The twelve of 149 attacked and one pilot, Squadron
Leader Paul Harris, who had led a flight on the 4 September raid to
the same area, claimed three hits:

> 'Among the German ships on which direct hits were obtained
> was one of the cruisers. Photographs were taken during the
> bombing.'

This Air Ministry statement carefully avoids saying that the photographs show the hits. What really happened was that a minesweeper

was sunk by an armour-piercing bomb that went right through without exploding. If there was any damage to cruisers, it was not significant enough to be noted in German records.

Rather more than one fighter appeared as the bombers were setting off for home, but there was no mass attack and no dogfight. The Messerschmitts rather hung back. One that did come in close was damaged by a 149 gunner, and another was shot down by Leading Aircraftman John Copley, tail gunner in a 38 Squadron Wimpy, with the fighter pilot surviving. Copley's DFM citation (*London Gazette* on 2 January 1940) stated:

> 'When his aircraft became isolated from the formation and was attacked by an enemy fighter aircraft from astern he opened fire at a range of approximately 150–200 yards, subsequently getting in at least two bursts of 20 rounds each at point blank range.'

The other encounter with the 149 Squadron Wellington also happened when it fell out of formation for a while. Putting these reports together, plus the news that other fighters were seemingly unwilling to come closer than 600 yards, reinforced the view in high places – and among some of the more gung-ho aircrew – that formations of bombers could defend themselves in daylight, especially against German fighter pilots who clearly lacked the King-and-country courage of the RAF.

The Secretary of State for Air, Sir Kingsley Wood, said in the House:

'We have a definite superiority over the Germans in the initiative and skill of our pilots ... the recent attack on German warships at Heligoland was yet another of the fine offensive actions of the war. It is significant that in the course of this flight the aircraft were engaged by some 20 Messerschmitt fighters, and two of these, which pressed home their attack, were driven down, and one of them certainly destroyed. This, I think, is a very striking tribute to the formidable gun defences of our bombers.'

Twelve more aircraft would be lost in training, often with fatalities, before the next real trial of strength on 14 December. The first reports in the British press, competing with extensive and victorious coverage of the Battle of the River Plate, had intense fighting over the Heligoland Bight in which four Messerschmitts and three RAF bombers were shot down. The German press had the fighters attacking 'twelve long-distance bombers of the newest type', shooting down eight of them while losing one of their own that 'had to come down in the sea'.

As more information emerged, it was noted that the bombers had sighted a battleship and a cruiser. Of course, the reports were based on accounts given by aircrew to intelligence officers. In the heat of battle, with no experience of such events, witnesses could not be expected to be perfectly accurate:

> 'Within a few moments, our aircraft were engaged by German fighters, and a desperate fight followed, in which the anti-aircraft guns of the warships joined. The fight lasted nearly half an hour. After 15 minutes a twin-engined German fighter fell in flames into the sea. A few minutes later another met the same fate, and these two were followed by a third and a fourth. A fifth dived vertically into the water.'

Four of the enemy planes were seen burning on the sea 'like enormous beacons'.

The twin-engined German fighters were the new Messerschmitt 110 and this was the RAF's first sight of them. They were a formidable foe for the Wellington, much faster, armed with cannon and machine guns, although not so hot against Spitfires and Hurricanes in daylight. The type would find its true metier as a night-fighter, and would score very heavily in the bomber war to come.

There were only four of them in the air on this day so, according to reports, the Wellington gunners got the lot, did they?

On 13 December HMS *Salmon*, an S-class submarine fresh from sinking a U-boat, had torpedoed two surface ships, the cruisers *Leipzig* and *Nürnberg*, which were returning from mine-laying duties off the Thames estuary. They were damaged but not fatally, and sailed on for home at Wilhelmshaven while their escort destroyers hunted the *Salmon*.

The weather was foul enough to defeat the first Bomber Command attempts to find the wounded ships so twelve Wellingtons of 99 Squadron were sent to have another shot. They carried crews of six with the extra gunner. No. 99 was based at Newmarket Heath on the racecourse, with billets in the grandstand, and their runway was the racetrack.

The squadron's only experience of the war, despite a number of standbys that never came to anything, was one trip on 30 October, to the same sea area. Bad weather again made that mission a waste of time except for some good on-the-job training in finding your home landing ground in the dark. They were to return to Mildenhall, rather than Newmarket Heath, for debriefing, but there was no ground control so they had to fly around trying to identify the right radio beacon.

Now 99 was on its second operation of the Second World War. Doing remarkably well to stick together, sometimes wave-hopping to get below the cloud, the squadron saw Wangerooge, the northernmost of the Friesian Islands. Ten minutes later they saw the cruisers and three destroyers, which opened up with a terrific flak barrage. The Wellingtons had armour-piercing bombs which had to be dropped from at least 2,000 feet. Orders were not to bomb unless that height could be achieved with targets in view. This was impossible on the day, so there was no point in taking risks with the flak. The squadron turned for home.

At this point, around 14.25, the first loss could have occurred. Bill Chorley's authoritative *Bomber Command Losses* has Sergeant Richard Brace being shot down by the ships' flak with all crew killed and no bodies found.

What happened next? The official view of the time was expressed by 'A Wing Commander':

> 'At this height (800 feet) effective bombing was impossible, and the Wellingtons were exposed to all the guns of the warships; it appears that the enemy used not only anti-aircraft guns but the long-range guns of the ships as well. In the confusion of battle two Wellingtons collided in mid-air, and others were seen to be shot down by anti-aircraft fire.'

By now, a strong force of Me109s, augmented by the four Me110s, was in the air and heading for the bombers, maybe warned of the formation by their new radar system Freya. It was widely accepted that the Germans didn't have radar and so no account of it was taken in aerial plans. When the fighters arrived, a running battle ensued in which, apparently, the bombers were the victors:

> 'The Messerschmitts made determined attacks from above and from below, but the Wellingtons kept formation and so used their guns in concert, directing cones of fire from their power-operated turrets. At least three Me110s and two Me109s were shot down; by this time it was growing dark, and as the fighters burnt on the surface of the water the sea was lit for miles around. There is some doubt about whether or not one bomber was shot down by fighters or by anti-aircraft fire. In all five Wellingtons were lost.'

Talk around the messes seems to have been that three or four fighters were shot down, while one Wellington went down in flames; another was hit by fighter fire and collided with a third, both falling. Two more disappeared after that and another, severely damaged, crashed at home.

In the clouds and confusion, added to the fury and novelty of the occasion, it is quite understandable that hindsight offers the only accurate viewpoint. Wellington N2870 was attacked by fighters; in taking evasive action Pilot Officer Norman Lewis flew his aircraft into N2911, pilot Flight Sergeant William Downey. Both went in. Two bodies were washed ashore from Downey's machine; all the rest are named at Runnymede. N2886, Flight Sergeant James Healey's machine was shot down in flames by fighters or ack-ack, all killed, no bodies.

The four twin-engined beacons burning on the sea were Wellingtons, not 110s.

N2956, Flying Officer John Cooper, was seen leaving the battlefield with undercart hanging down but no trace was ever found of aircraft or men. Flight Lieutenant Eugene Hetherington, a New Zealander, nursed his badly damaged craft almost home but crashed on trying to land, killing himself and two others.

On the plus side, the rear gunner in the lead aircraft, Corporal Alexander Bickerstaff, claimed a Me109 and he was right. His DFM citation in the *London Gazette* of 2 January 1940, stated:

'(A Messerschmitt) engaged the leader's aircraft at extremely close range. Corporal Bickerstaff quickly brought his guns to bear and directed a cool and accurate fire, his tracer being seen to pass directly through the pilot's position before the enemy aircraft burst into flames and crashed into the sea.'

That pilot was named by the Germans as killed, Leutnant Brankmeier. The good corporal is to be especially commended for his defence of his Wellington, because it was flown by Squadron Leader Andrew McKee, later OC 9 Squadron, even later Air Marshal Sir Andrew, KCB, CBE, DSO, DFC, AFC, with second pilot Wingco John Griffiths, OC 99 Squadron. Griffiths was awarded the DFC for this action. As Group Captain, he would be killed in a flying accident on 9 May 1945, the day after VE Day.

Air Commodore Bottomley, the staff officer charged with analysing this disaster in which half the force was lost, said that 'it seems almost possible to assume' that the fighters were not responsible for any of the bomber losses. Having thus almost assumed, and allowing for half an hour's fighter attacks, he then ascribed the bombers' invulnerability to rigid formation flying while under fire.

In other words: we lost six out of twelve of our Wellingtons to anti-aircraft fire from the ships, but the fighters didn't bother us, so let's keep attacking the ships.

The German pilots claimed five Wellingtons plus one probable, admitting one Me109 lost and one damaged. As the navy flak gunners made no claims, perhaps those pilots were correct and Brace and crew were also their victims, and the probable was Flight Lieutenant Hetherington's machine.

In *The Luftwaffe War Diaries* the weather that day is described as 'filthy: Snow and rain, with cloud pockets right down on the sea'. Oberstleutnant Carl Schumacher, OC fighter group JG1, based at Jever in East Friesland, gave his reason for the fighters' success:

'Most of von Bülow's fighter pilots were ex naval men. In that weather any normal unit would have made a mess of it, and come home empty-handed.'

Major Harry von Bülow commanded a squadron of Me109s based on Wangerooge.

Senior RAF commanders agreed that in view of the achievements of this operation, another should be mounted as soon as could be, with the proviso that aircraft must attack from 10,000 feet above the flak. It cannot have been considered relevant that no Wellington crew, in practice or anger, in cloud or clear skies, had ever hit anything as small as a ship with a bomb from 10,000 feet, much less one that was steaming along and possibly taking evasive action.

Prime Minister Chamberlain went to France on 15 December to lunch with French VIPs but also to inspect our fighting men. Mick Maguire, armourer with 88 Squadron, remembered it well:

> 'The trouble with the Fairey Battle was that it was a flying fire hazard when loaded, and the hazard was the petrol. There were no self-sealing tanks as far as the RAF was concerned. We had a Dornier in the back of a hangar that a Hurricane had shot down and we made a point of showing it to the Prime Minister when he came to see us. He looked like something from 1918, in his gaiters and deerstalker hat and starched wing collar. Maybe that explained why things hadn't moved on so much in the air force since then. Anyway, Warrant Officer Pape was making the point that this German aircraft had self-sealing fuel tanks, and Chamberlain said in his squeaky voice, "We must have some of these, Mr Pape". We fell about laughing, but it wasn't funny really.
>
> 'The Battle generally carried four 250 pounders, or sometimes some 40 pounders instead of one of the 250s. We had winches and gear to load them in but it was easier to get our strongest man to bend over beneath the aircraft, and then put a 250 on his back. He pushed upwards and click, in it went. We came unstuck with this technique with an aircraft which had been spraying coloured water to test how clouds of smoke, or poison gas, might behave. Our strong man Bill Jones got underneath and arched his back to take the empty tank while someone in the cockpit pressed the release. Only problem was it was a full one, and Bill was flattened.'

CHAPTER 4

The Battle of Heligoland

Air Vice Marshal John Baldwin, known as Jackie, had been called out of retirement to command 3 Group of Bomber Command. He was keen on another attack against warships, and his senior colleagues agreed. He called a meeting at Mildenhall on 17 December at 19.00 hours, attended by squadron COs and flight commanders of 9, 37 and 149 Squadrons. Twenty-four Wellingtons were to look for warships in the Schillig Roads. If none were found, then they were to look at Wilhelmshaven where, it was believed, lay the battlecruisers *Scharnhorst* and *Gneisenau* and many other warships. Baldwin emphasised the vital importance of formation discipline.

They were to fly in a shape usually called a diamond but really it looked more like a cross or, indeed, a rather stumpy aircraft. Up front would be two sections of three in vic, all 149 Squadron, with Wingco Richard Kellett and his two wingmen in the lead. Behind them, to the right and 500 feet above, were two more sections also in vic, being three of 149 and three of 9. Similarly, but to the left and above, were six of No. 9 arranged in the same way. Bringing up the rear, 1,000 feet above Kellett, in line astern and stepped down, were two rows of three, all of 37 Squadron.

There had been no time for the squadrons to practise this. On the Rhyl exercise, 9 and 37 had flown together; they had also co-operated on one sea sweep, but 149 had not flown with either. In 9 and 37, they were not all the same crews anyway. No. 37 had been on ops but had had no experience of meeting the enemy – fighters or flak – and Kellett, although he'd led the 3 December raid, was new to his squadron.

In the morning, Baldwin told the assembled officers, they were to stand by at two hours readiness from 07.30. If the attack went ahead

89

they were to ensure that none of their bombs fell on land or on merchant ships. Confirmation of the op would come after a recce flight to determine the weather over the target, in which case they would rendezvous over King's Lynn.

The weather report turned out to be favourable: patchy cloud. There was no intelligence report on the fighter strength around the target area, and there was a general feeling that the Germans were a bit leery anyway. In fact, Schumacher had little short of a hundred Me109s and 110s that could be scrambled in minutes, flown by men who were very keen indeed to shoot down a Tommy or two.

At around 09.00, nine Wellingtons of 9 Squadron took off from Honington. A few minutes later, the nine of 149 Squadron left Mildenhall, while the six of 37 Squadron were delayed, missed the RV over King's Lynn and had to motor to catch up. These were all Mark IA Wellingtons with hydraulic, rotating gun turrets, armour protecting the starboard fuel tanks but, for some bizarre reason, not the port tanks and not yet with self-sealing tanks at all, or proper, efficient heating for the crew. It happened to be an exceptionally cold day in an exceptionally cold winter. Inside a draughty Wellington, it seemed that there could be nowhere as cold as this.

The plan was to fly at 14,000 feet, north-east to latitude 55°, well to the north of the target area; turn right, as it were, along the latitude line, then right again, south, towards their destination. The cloud hid them for much of the way but, some two hours into the journey, it began to thin. The front man of the second section of the leading group had engine trouble and could not keep station. He signalled his predicament. One of his wingmen got the message and joined up with Kellett. The other turned away for home with his leader.

The twenty-two flew on, not yet in sight of land, and the cloud vanished. Turning south in a clear blue sky that they seemed to have all to themselves, dustbin turrets were lowered and manned, just in case, although they expected their route, away from known positions of flak ships, to give them the advantage of surprise.

They knew nothing of radar – or radio location as it was then called. On Heligoland a German navy operator, watching on his recently delivered Freya radar set, was near incredulous as his new-fangled machine told him that a formation of aircraft was about seventy miles away. At the Luftwaffe experimental station on Wangerooge, the Freya operator saw the same thing and calculated the hostiles' distance as 113 kilometres, or twenty minutes' flying time.

They had to be hostiles. There were no German aircraft aloft in that region. The message from Heligoland went round the houses and back through naval exchanges before reaching Schumacher's HQ twenty minutes later, where it was disregarded as duff gen from the incompetent sailor boys. The Wangerooge message went direct, but wasn't believed. The new kit was showing seagulls. It was a beautiful day. The Tommies wouldn't come in this weather.

Observers on the ground with binoculars soon confirmed the radar reports – better than that, double confirmed them, sighting forty-four bombers – and the fighters scrambled. First up was a night-fighter squadron, six Me109s of JG26 led by Staffelkapitän 'Macki' Steinhoff, who would become a formidable ace in the Battle of Britain.

Other future top scorers there that day were Gordon Gollob, who would retire from the air with 150 claimed kills, and Helmut Lent, destined to be one of the two most successful night-fighter pilots in the Luftwaffe. On this day Lent, with only one Polish victory to his credit so far, refuelling and impatient after returning from a patrol, famously took off with his armourer still on the wing changing an ammunition drum. The armourer, Paul Mahle, slid off and rolled to safety, which was one of the most unfortunate survivals of the war for Bomber Command. In 1943, he would develop the upward-firing cannon system known as *Schrägemusik* (slanted music), which accounted for so many hundreds of Lancasters and Halifaxes and their crews. If only Lent had been a little more impatient.

In this, the biggest air battle any of the participants had ever seen or heard about, the Germans faced an enemy who had bravery, instincts and common sense but no real notion of air fighting. The assumption was that the fighters would come in from behind; there had been no training in how a Wellington might deal with a smaller, faster, better armed and more acrobatic foe who did something unexpected.

The 110s had 20mm cannon, effective at 600 yards, beyond the range of the Wellington's machine-gun turrets. The fighter pilots knew that if they dived in from the side, those machine guns couldn't get to them anyway, while nobody in the RAF – officially at least – had considered such beam attacks a serious possibility.

The Wellington pilots had no tactic other than sticking together in formation as recommended after the Rhyl exercise, and/or hiding in the clouds, but there were no clouds. The clouds had gone.

The formation flew on searching for warships and finding only the forbidden merchantmen until Wilhelmshaven, where there were warships all right including *Scharnhorst* and *Gneisenau*, but they were forbidden too, tied up at the quay. Bombs dropped on them could easily hit on land, and that was strictly against orders. The ships had no restrictions on their own activities; the anti-aircraft barrage coming from them was thick and angry. With heavy flak exploding in black thunderballs all around, Sergeant Frank Petts was finding life difficult.

> 'I was the outside-left of the whole team and in our wide turn over the water it was increasingly hard to keep up. Even at full throttle and full revs on the props I was lagging, then the flak stopped and there were the fighters, about forty of them. Hoping to gain some speed I dropped my bombs, which were four 500lb general purpose, quite unsuitable anyway for trying to sink battleships.'

For everyone that day it was new experience, the biggest, fiercest, most appallingly deadly rumble anybody had witnessed so far in this war. Petts:

> 'LAC Balch on the front guns got a fighter. It was a Me109, sweeping wide, possibly looking to come in on the leading aircraft. I saw Balch's first burst take off part of the cockpit and his second hit in the same area. The Messerschmitt went into a catastrophic dive pouring white smoke. By now I'd decided I'd never keep up and Ginger Heathcote (second pilot) said we could drop back and join the 37 Squadron six at the rear. Thank goodness I didn't.'

The bombers tried to keep together for support but it proved impossible. The formation was now all over the place and, without the combined defences of the group, the fighters had it even easier.

The 9 Squadron section of six had become detached from the rest. In came the 110s. Flying Officer John Challes's machine was shot to pieces in mid-air; Flying Officer Douglas Allison was last seen heading for home with an engine in flames; Pilot Officer Eric Lines was not seen at all. Lamb's replacement, Squadron Leader Archibald Guthrie, went into the sea on fire but got a 110 which force-landed. Every man was killed in these four Wellington losses.

It so nearly could have been even worse. Petts:

'I turned about 40 degrees to starboard and headed full pelt for the waves. I was fairly well occupied with matters arising but I did notice the needle on my ASI reaching one o'clock second time around, which I later worked out meant 300 miles an hour.'

The Pegasus-engined Mark IA Wellington had a specified maximum speed of 265mph, and Petts was not the only one in that aircraft wondering how much faster they could go without something falling off. A fighter had attacked just before the dive and there were more during the dive, and as Petts pulled out of it at sea level, three Me110s settled in behind him. This was a particularly exciting time for Bob Kemp in the dustbin turret. In full kit he was a tight fit in there, and if the Germans didn't get him he was liable to be knocked off the aircraft by an unsuspecting porpoise. Petts:

'We had an agreed drill for stern attacks. Robertson in the rear turret called it. ''There's one coming in,'' he'd say. ''He's coming . . . get ready, get ready . . . back! Back!'' I'd slam the throttles shut and the pitch levers to full coarse. Our guns would be firing, there'd be enemy tracer past the windows and, with any luck, an enemy aircraft past us too. ''OK, he's gone,'' somebody would say, and we'd be back to full speed ahead. My gunners claimed three 110s and two 109s that day. I could confirm with my own eyes Balch's 109 and a 110 he got. The others I couldn't say for sure. Robertson said he'd had a go at that 110 with no effect and one of its crew had made a rude gesture at him. As we throttled back, the 110 was suddenly in front and Balch gave him the full benefit.'

By now two of Petts's gunners were wounded; Balch's was only a graze on his foot but Kemp had a very nasty thigh wound and was losing a lot of blood. Second pilot Heathcote managed to prise him out of his dustbin and treat him on the rest bed. The ammunition was gone anyway, the aircraft was full of holes and the starboard engine showed zero oil pressure. At least the fire in the starboard wing had gone out. Petts found he could climb gently to 1,000 feet and set a course of 270°. With no clue where they were, he and Ginger Heathcote reasoned that if they went due west they should hit the UK somewhere.

Similar alarms, battles and mayhem were happening to the rest of the formation. Flying Officer James Speirs's machine, one of Kellett's wingmen, was shot up by a 110 and exploded. Flying Officer Michael Briden's Wimpy, a flying wreck with fuel leaks, struggled along with the rest of 149 and some of No. 9 as they got themselves out of the fighters' range and set course for home. Briden didn't make it. Watched by his friends and colleagues, he made the perfect ditching about fifty miles off Cromer, but searches by Cromer lifeboat and others found no trace.

In the same formation as Briden, the starboard six led by Squadron Leader Harris of 149, Sergeant Jack Ramshaw's machine of No. 9 was also hit in the wings but claimed two Messerschmitts downed by w/opAG Leading Aircraftman Walter Lilley, a lad of twenty-one from Kippax in Yorkshire. Aircraftman First Class Charles Driver, a member of the squadron's ground crew acting as temporary air gunner for the second time, was in the front turret. He watched in horror as half of it was shot away, his guns were rendered u/s and a fire broke out behind him. He beat the fire out and went to help his mate Walter at the back who was mortally wounded. Driver laid him on the aircraft floor and went to the skipper's aid. Petrol was leaking, the pumps weren't working properly and the second pilot, Sergeant Bob Hewitt had a wound in his right arm. Driver began pumping petrol by hand as Ramshaw headed for home. They lost height steadily and were almost in the sea by the time they saw the English coast. Driver kept pumping while the pilot ditched as near as he could to a trawler he'd spotted.

Trawler skipper Sinclair took the observer, Leading Aircraftman Conolly and Ramshaw aboard his vessel *Erillas* without difficulty. Bob Hewitt fell in the December waves. Driver pulled him out and they too boarded the trawler and set off for the shore and Grimsby

Veteran of the Brunsbüttel raid and survivor of Heligoland, pilot Sergeant Tom Purdy sits with his back to the snooker table in the sergeants' mess. As Warrant Officer Purdy DFM, he was killed with 57 Squadron, 28 December 1941.

Hospital. Leading Aircraftman Walter Lilley had fought his heart out and went down with his aircraft.

For the rest of 9 Squadron, Flight Lieutenant Peter Grant and Sergeant Tom Purdy, both veterans of the 4 September battle so long ago, were the only two pilots to land at Honington base. Four of the 9 Squadron port formation of six had fallen. The other two staggered in to emergency landings. Sergeant Petts, starting from nowhere, heading due west and spotting Butlin's camp at Skegness, came in at Sutton Bridge with two wounded crew, his starboard wing badly shot up and having been on fire, and the starboard side of the fuselage 'freely peppered', as they called it then.

Flying Officer Bill Macrae, who had been Guthrie's wingman in the leading section of the port six, also couldn't make Honington and landed at North Coates Fittes, with patterns of holes in the wings and, to the dismay of rear gunner, Leading Aircraftman Frank Horry, in large parts of the tail section, plus a holed fuel tank and the fuselage peppered.

It was something of a miracle that Petts and Macrae got back, a miracle ascribable equally to crew and machine, and a double miracle that nobody in Macrae's ship was hit, so many were his bullet holes.

Now out of their unorthodox stepped formation – they obviously hadn't heard about 9 Squadron's fatal experiment with it – 37 Squadron's six emerged from the flak some way behind everyone else, still flying in their three pairs but in line astern. One pilot went to open his bomb doors to jettison, selected master hydraulic cock 'on' without realising he had flaps selected 'down', and gave himself a massive upward surge just as a flock of Me110s came hurtling in, led by Helmut Lent.

First to go down was the front man, Squadron Leader Ian Hue-Williams, raked by cannon fire from a Me110 and hitting the sea with wings on fire. His number two, Flying Officer Lemon – he who had just had the gravity-defying incident with bomb doors and flaps – was alone and pursued by two Me109s. As they dived and raced at zero feet across the waves, the Wellington crew were rewarded with the sight of one of the fighters dipping his wing in the sea and disappearing in spectacular fashion. The other Messerschmitt decided that the better part of valour was discretion and flew away.

Lemon flew very low all the way home and waited for the others to come back.

Flying Officer Peter Wimberley was the only survivor of his ditching, finished off by Lent after others had already damaged the bomber beyond fighting back. Sergeant Herbert Ruse, another Lent victim, had two crew killed in the attack and force-landed on the sand dunes of Borkum. Ruse, like most of them, had dropped his bombs to give him extra speed and agility. The Germans were astonished to find no bombs aboard because they were sure none had been dropped, on targets or jettisoned.

According to *The Luftwaffe War Diaries*, Wimberley, Ruse and the other POWs accounted for the lack of bombs by saying they hadn't been carrying any. It wasn't a raid at all, but a training and reconnaissance flight, with extra crewmen aboard for the experience.

Flying Officer Arthur Thompson had his tail shot right off and hit the sea with all men killed. Flying Officer Oliver Lewis's craft broke up in mid-air, helpless under a fighter's sustained attacks. The tail gunner survived the crash but died of his wounds.

So, Lemon and all at RAF Feltwell, home of 37 Squadron, waited in vain.

Of the twenty-two Wellingtons that reached the target, twelve were lost with fifty-eight crew dead and five POWs, while German aircrew claimed thirty-four out of forty-four Wellingtons downed, later reduced to twenty-seven.

The ten returning Wellington crews claimed six 110s and six 109s. The actual score was no 110s although nine were damaged of which two force-landed, and two 109s shot down plus one force-landed. This was war as it had never been experienced before – terrifying, electrifying, shocking and, not surprisingly, liable to produce unreliable witnesses.

The papers were no more reliable:

> 'Air Battle in Bight. 12 Enemy Craft Shot Down. The Air Ministry announced last night that a bomber formation of the R.A.F reconnoitred the Heligoland Bight area yesterday afternoon with the object of attacking any enemy warships found at sea.
>
> 'No warships were encountered at sea, but the bombers met strong fighter forces.
>
> 'Fierce fighting followed and 12 Messerschmitts were shot down. Seven of our bombers are at present unaccounted for.'

The German news agency reported thirty-four 'of the most modern battle aeroplanes' shot down for the loss of two of their own. Two British crews were taken prisoner while the German pilots parachuted to safety and parts of the British planes were washed ashore.

Another report from the fatherland gave fifty-two as the number of bombers engaged, with at least forty going down. Oberstleutnant Schumacher, the senior officer on the German side of the fight, gave a press conference in which he praised the British pilots as brave and enterprising – as well as the sound construction of the German aircraft, some of which had come home with thirty-five bullet holes, and some with one engine out of action. He confirmed that losses were two Me109s.

In his written report, he said that damage to his fighters was due to 'the tight formation and excellent rear-gunners', but that 'maintenance of formation and rigid adherence to course made them easy targets to find.'

A reflective piece by The Times *Aeronautical Correspondent asked if all this bomber activity was really worthwhile: 'There have been since the outbreak of war a great many air operations the purpose of which is obscure. On all these occasions proof has been given of the fine fighting spirit of the Royal Air Force officers and men, and of the technical excellence of their equipment. But the question has been asked if an adequate return is being secured for the losses incurred. The task of the bombers in seeking to obtain results (against warships rather than land targets) is multiplied in difficulty many times over, while the task of the defences which are set up against it is facilitated.'*

Home news, December 1939.

'Norfolk turkeys are fetching 2s 4d a pound at Smithfield; other turkeys and geese at 2s. 2d and 2s.'

'It has been announced that the price of petrol will shortly rise by a halfpenny a gallon to 1s 10d.'

Another commander, Hauptman Reinecke, wrote:

'The Me110 is easily capable of catching and overtaking this English type even with the latter at full boost. This provides scope for multiple attacks from any quarter, including frontal beam. This attack can be very effective if the enemy aircraft is allowed to fly into the cone of fire. The Wellington is very inflammable and burns readily.'

Petts was mentioned in despatches; his DFM would come later. Harris and his second pilot, Pilot Officer Harome Innes, and Macrae had the DFC. Flight Lieutenant Grant and Leading Aircraftman Conolly were MID. Jack Ramshaw had the DFM, as did his front gunner, an eighteen-year-old fitter/rigger seconded to the job, Aircraftman First Class Charles Driver. He would stay as groundcrew for another eighteen months before taking up gunning full time, and would eventually be commissioned. Harris's rear gunner Aircraftman First Class James Mullineaux had the DFM, as did Flying Officer Hugh Bulloch's gunner Leading Aircraftman Walter Greig.

Place.	Date.	Time.	Summary of Events.	References to Appendices.
HONINGTON.	18/12.		Amendment to Form B.60 received.	App. "H".
			H.Q. 3 Group signal Ops.923 dated 17/12 detailed No. 3 Squadron to stand by for coastal duties on 18th December - 9 aircraft to participate and to carry	
		0900	No. 5 Series Bombs. Squadron to stand-by at 2 hour's notice from 0730 hours. Nine Wellington aircraft took off for Operations in accordance with H.Q. 3 Group Form B.60.	
		1600	Two Wellington aircraft N.2964 (D) and N.2981(F) landed	
		1730	Wellington 'A. N.2871 (B) landed at(North Coates.) NORTH COATES.	
		1730	Wellington 'A. N.2973.(C) landed at(Sutton Bridge) 54675 L.AC. BALCH, G., SUTTON BRIDGE.	
			and 551263. AC.1. KEMP, F.S. reported wounded in the crew of N.2873.	App. "H".
			Complete crews of N.2872.,N.2983., N.2941., N.2939., and N.2940. reported on Casualty Signal as Missing.	
			For detailed crews and report see relevant Form 541.	
			Local Weather. Wind E.N.E. 10-20 mph. Mainly overcast. Cloud mainly 10/10 1-2000 feet Visibility: 2-4 miles.	
HONINGTON.	19/12.	1150	It was reported that the undermentioned crew of N.2983 had been picked up in the North Sea and were in GRIMSBY HOSPITAL.	
			562599. Sgt. RAMSHAW, J.R. 521236. Sgt. R.HEWITT. 531023. L.AC. CONNLY, P.J. 628742. AC.1. DRIVER, C.R.	
			No news was received of: 538024. L.AC. WILLLEY the remaining member of the crew. Local Weather. Cloud mainly 10/10 decreasing to Nil after 1900 hours. Wind N.W. 5-10 mph. Weather cloudy. Visibility : 2-4 miles.	

Operations Record Book of No. 9 Squadron, the Battle of Heligoland.

Place.	Date.	Time.	Summary of Events.	References to Appendices.
HONINGTON.	20/12.		Information received that 531236. Sgt. P. HEWISON. 2nd pilot of N.2983 had gunshot wound in right arm and had been transferred to R.A.F. HOSPITAL, CRANWELL. Air Ministry signal P.917 dated 19.12.39. stated that 532024 L.AC. W.LILLEY rear gunner of N.2983 had been killed in action 18th December, 1939. 39198. FLIGHT LIEUTENANT J.W.FORDHAM and S/Ldr. L.E.JARMAN posted to the Squadron. Authority received for 74466 PILOT OFFICER A.N.DAVID DAVER/ASD. to be posted to the Squadron with effect from 30th October 1939 to fill post as ASSISTANT ADJUTANT.	App. "J". App. "M".
HONINGTON.	21/12.	0920.	AIR CHIEF MARSHALL SIR EDGAR R. LUDLOW-HEWITT, K.C.B. C.M.G., D.S.O., M.C. arrived to interview crews of aircraft who participated in operations on the 18th December, 1939. The undermentioned officers and airmen were recommended for the immediate awards as stated : 37801. F/Lt. I.P.GRANT. D.F.C. 39089. F/O. W.J.MACRAE. D.F.C. 563599. Sgt. J.FAWSHAW. D.F.M. 626752. AC.1. C.P.DRIVER. D.F.M. The undermentioned airmen were recommended as worthy of Mention in Despatches 565932. Sgt. P.C.PETTS. 551023. L.AC. D. CONOLLY. Local Weather E.Wind. less than 10 mph. Cloudy with scattered showers. Visibility poor.	

OPERATIONS RECORD BOOK.

DETAIL OF WORK CARRIED OUT

From ....0855.. hrs. ....18../..12../..39..... to ....1600..hrs. ..18../..12../..39..

By ....No. 9. Squadron......

No. of pages used for day........

Aircraft Type and No.	Crew.	Duty.	Time Up.	Time Down.	Remarks.	References.
Wellington Mark. 1A.						
N.2941.	P/Off. D.R.ALLISON. P/Off. D.C.BAILEY. Sgt. J.A.PRISCER. 580848. 591698. Sgt. J.P.TURNBULL. 567249. Cpl. R.T.BLACK. 533017. L.AC. A.C.COODENOUCH.		0855	–	Failed to return. Reported Missing p.m. 18.12.39.	
N. 2939.	F/Off. J.T.I.CHALLES. P/Off. A.H.R.BOURNE. 580718. Sgt. F.M.MASON. 524025. Sgt. T.H.ENGLISH. 566740. L.AC. C.E.COX. 531958. AC.1. A.TELFERR.		0855	–	Failed to return. Reported Missing p.m. 18.12.39.	
N.2940.	P/Off. E.F.LINES. 563436. F/Sgt. BRAPNSIDE. A.K. 551731. AC.1. E.M.C.POLHILL. 588708. L.AC. A.M.DICKIE. 627354. AC.2. C.WALKER.		0855.	–	Failed to return. Reported Missing p.m. 18.12.39.	

The men left from this calamity were interviewed by the RAF's Commander-in-Chief, Air Chief Marshal Sir Edgar R. Ludlow-Hewitt KCB, CMG, DSO, MC. Group Captain Hugh Pughe-Lloyd MC, DFC, OC 9 Squadron at the start of the war, was now a 3 Group staff officer. He criticised the route taken to the target, running so far down the coast, 'giving the enemy all the warning he could get'.

Like the modern sports team defeated by a large margin, the senior commanders tried to take some positives out of the action.

Kellet's front runners, four of them as it panned out, had stuck together, lost only one and shot down many of the enemy, as then thought. The top brass still didn't know about the Freya radar. Had

its operators been believed sooner, the bombers who were first in and first out may not have been so unscathed.

The two that ditched would have had enough petrol to make it home if they had had self-sealing fuel tanks and armour in the port wing. Well, at least we can learn from that. Pity about the men who died, but there you are.

Baldwin was so sure that tight formation flying had saved the home-comers, that he blamed the losses on the dead commanders of 9 and 37 Squadrons, Guthrie and Hue-Williams who, in his view, had shown poor leadership in flying too far ahead of their followers. Ludlow-Hewitt said this was a 'great and unforgivable crime', and that formations, unshaken under attack, were like the Thin Red Line of yore.

AC1 Charles Driver was front gunner in Jack Ramshaw's Wellington at the Battle of Heligoland. After being fished out of the sea, eighteen-year-old Driver was awarded the DFM.

How many more Wellingtons would have to be shot down, and how many more men would have to die, before it was realised that Wellingtons in daylight were not a good idea? The answer would come very soon.

Official instructions were that, for the moment, if any German ships were spotted out at sea, Squadrons Nos 38 and 115 would have to deal with them as a consequence of operational losses suffered by other squadrons.

Overheard in the officers' mess after the 18 December raid: 'The air was so thick with lead that I had to blind fly for ten minutes.'

CHAPTER 5

Norway in the Spring

On the day that Ludlow-Hewitt was interviewing survivors of Wilhelmshaven, 21 December, two Hampdens of 44 Squadron, returning from a recce off Norway, were shot down off the Berwickshire coast. The attackers were not Messerschmitts but Spitfires of 602 Squadron charged with defending Scotland against air raids. One man was killed, w/opAG Leading Aircraftman Terrance Gibbin. The other seven were pulled out of the sea by local fishermen. Another Hampden, 49 Squadron, coming back to Scampton from a recce, ran out of petrol and crashed in Northumberland, killing two.

Two Hampdens of 44 Squadron, returning from a recce off Norway, were shot down off the Berwickshire coast, 21 December 1939, by Spitfires of 602 Squadron.

105

A Blenheim of 107 Squadron, returning to the scene of their devastation on 4 September and looking for shipping yet again in the Schillig Roads, was lost without trace.

And so the old year went out in a flurry of snow and a lack of success. Squadrons were told to stand by for sea sweeps, and then told to stand down. When one such sweep went ahead, it finally convinced the senior commanders that Wellingtons could not defeat Me110s, no matter how close they kept formation.

Hugh Bulloch, 149 Squadron, was designated leader of a section of three. Harome Innes, now a skipper, and Sergeant John Morrice were his wingmen in an expedition captained entirely by Scotsmen. They had been fitted by now with armour plate in the port wing and with self-sealing fuel tanks. Despite these marked advantages over the Wellington 1As of 18 December, the Me110s still proved superior to the Wimpys and only Innes came back. He had seen Bulloch's machine on fire as it hit the sea, but didn't know what happened to Morrice. He and his gunners claimed two 110s destroyed out of the dozen or so that attacked.

German reports show that four Me110s mounted a surprise attack. Bulloch and Morrice were shot down in flames and two of the 110s were damaged – badly enough to have to get home on one engine. That Innes didn't make a third victim can only be due to the skill and determination of the pilot, skimming the waves as he ran for it, and the gunners. Navigator Sergeant Austin in the dustbin turret said he fired 3,000 rounds.

We cannot be sure that this was the incident that caused Baldwin and Ludlow-Hewitt to change their minds. We do know that no more Wellingtons went in daylight to look for ships around Heligoland, and that Ludlow-Hewitt was replaced as C-in-C by Charles Portal in April 1940.

The puzzle remains of why the bombers were doing this in the first place. Traditionally the RAF had no interest in sinking ships, although that was the given purpose of the German Bight raids. Bomber Command had no torpedo-carrying aircraft, which was the usual weapon against warships, and no aircraft designed as dive-bombers. A dive-bomber, screaming in at top speed and releasing armour-piercing bombs at the last moment, was the other method by which success might be achieved.

Conventional bombing at low level was tried and found to be worse than useless. At high level, there was no possibility of hitting a moving target. So, what was it all about?

From correspondence between Ludlow-Hewitt and Baldwin it seems that a combination of training, intelligence gathering and combat-hardening was the answer. It was really a First World War, common-sense idea to send new crews on an op or two where they could experience flak and maybe fighters but not with too high a risk. The same idea would be employed later in this war, when bomber crews would be sent to a target on the French coast for their first op before being ordered next night to Berlin.

In 1939 nobody knew how aerial warfare would work out. There were plenty of theories but the only way to prove any of them was to go and do it. Unfortunately, rather than sending the boys across the Channel to bomb a harbour the only option was to send them far away on a long journey that would test everything about the aircraft and the crew, to a place much more heavily defended than had been realised. Combining the two operations of 14 and 18 December, the loss rate was fifty per cent.

This was the first plain showing of the conundrum that Bomber Command would never solve. Experienced crews were much more likely to return, much less likely to be lost. But how do you get the experience?

Despite the wrigglings of the senior commanders – we had no choice, the Germans were better than we thought, the leaders should have kept formation, it wasn't our fault – 1939 was not all in vain. A lesson was learned. It was noticed that, while the Wellingtons and Blenheims and Hampdens and Battles were being shot down in daylight, the Whitleys were almost always coming home in the night. Guy Gibson:

'The next few weeks were spent in concentrated night flying training. Off we would go over the snow-covered fields of England, map-reading our way from here to there at 2,000 feet; sometimes we would lose our way, but with each practice we got better and better. It seemed now that Hampden squadrons were going to be used for night raiding only; they were too vulnerable in daylight.'

Regardless of any lessons learned, the ship searches carried on through the first three weeks of January 1940. Almost 200 sorties were flown, mostly by Blenheims and Wellingtons which never saw any ships and never dropped any bombs. Contact with the Messerschmitts was rare; the bombers were instructed not to go near the coast except in cloud. Fighters were met twice, by 149 Squadron on 2 January as we have seen, and by 110 Squadron on 10 January. The result of the latter encounter was one Blenheim exploding as it hit the water with all crew killed, and two badly damaged Blenheims crashing at home with no one killed. The fighters were the longer range Me110s and once again Ken Doran DFC, winner of one of the first two medals of the war and famous for his washing, was in among it as acting Squadron Leader. He achieved another first for the Second World War – a Bar to his DFC. *London Gazette*, 30 January 1940:

> 'This officer was the leader of a formation of bomber aircraft which was attacked by enemy fighters over the North Sea. By his clever tactics and gallant leadership he success-fully maintained a close defensive formation throughout the engagement, two of the fighter aircraft being compelled to break off the fight, a third being shot down in flames into the sea, and the remainder eventually abandoning the attack. Although one of our aircraft was lost and a second returned to its base, Squadron Leader Doran showed great deter-mination in leading the remaining aircraft a distance of about 130 miles further on to his objective.'

Leading Aircraftman John Tippett, w/opAG in the tail-end Charlie of the formation, received the DFM, having 'greatly assisted in repelling the enemy attacks throughout the engagement'. His was one of the two that crash-landed at home, so Tippet had that to endure as well.

The nickelling raids carried on too, with a slight difference. Hampdens and Wellingtons were employed as well as the faithful Whitleys. This, with the extra night training, surely indicated a change of operational direction for bomber Groups 3 and 5, previously intended for daylight flying.

One such op on 19 January featured two Wellingtons of 9 Squadron headed for Hamburg, Bremen, Hannover and Brunswick. The two took off together at 16.52. Sgt Leeke was home at 22.55; the other, not home for another hour, was captained by Wing Commander Andrew McKee AFC (Air Force Cross, awarded for gallantry on non-operational flights). Presumably he had got lost or had visited all the target cities.

The future Air Marshal and knight was quite a character. Andrew McKee was a New Zealander, born 10 January 1902 at Oxford, Canterbury. From the moment he joined the RAF in January 1927 he

Squadron Leader with 99 Squadron, Wing Commander OC 9 Squadron, Andrew McKee was ever known as 'Square', for obvious reasons. He is seen here in later life as Sir Andrew, Air Marshal.

was known as 'Square' McKee, a simple reference to his personal geometry – his height of 5ft 5in being observed as equal to his width.

He began in wild times on the North West Frontier with kings coming and going in Kabul and rebellions against the British in Waziristan, Peshawar and elsewhere, flying 27 Squadron's DH9A and Westland Wapiti. With No. 99 he had the Handley Page Hinaidi and the Heyford. At 58 Squadron he had the Vickers Virginia, including the Mark VIII with the open gun turrets on the wings, and back at 99 again, the Wellington. Frank Petts:

> (after Wilhelmshaven) 'We had ten days' special leave and returned to find a new flight commander and a new squadron CO. After Brunsbüttel and Wilhelmshaven there was a feeling, voiced mostly by the sergeant pilots, that we knew more about the war than either of these officers.'

Not entirely fair, Frank. McKee had had the experience of 14 December with 99 Squadron and was a leader from the front – an 'up-and-at-'em' type. The flight commander, Squadron Leader M. E. Jarman – later Air Commodore DFC and three times MID – indeed had had no combat experience so far. He was another Kiwi and had been in various training and engineering-officer posts since 1930. But where was Petts going to find a flight commander who could say he had been shot at by Me110s? There were not so many around.

Snow was on its way and from 20 January for almost four weeks there were no night ops. Daytime sea sweeps continued until the start of February with veterans Petts, Ramshaw, Macrae and Bowen finding nothing as usual. Jarman had another new boy as second pilot, Flying Officer Tom Kirby-Green, whose name would one day appear on the most shameful list of POWs every compiled by the Germans.

Over in France, there was only training and exercises for the Fairey Battles. They tried dive-bombing and worked out hopeful schemes for dealing with fighter attacks, but even that came to a stop when the snow fell. An airfield much further south, at St Laurent la Salanque, near Perpignan, became a temporary base for more training. They would have to wait until March for action, when reconnaissance flights were resumed.

A Fairey Battle of 88 Squadron, ready for take off in the snows of Mourmelon-le-Grand, France in early 1940.

The sea sweeps started again. Eighteen Wellingtons went, 11 February, and twelve two days later. ORB, 9 Squadron:

'10.30. Telephonic communication from Group confirmed Routine Sweep to be carried out at Station Commander's discretion. 11.06, three aircraft took off for Routine Sweep. 14.15 all aircraft returned.'

Excitement mounted a few days later. ORB, 9 Squadron:

'Squadron standing by for special operation in accordance with telephone message consequent upon observation made by Whitley at 01.00 hours. Whitley observed four large warships, two of which appeared to be battle cruisers. Three-four miles south of Heligoland a line of nine or ten warships of which two or three at the northern end were probably destroyers and one vessel which appeared to be an ice breaker was seen about one mile north of this line. All ships were surrounded by ice which extended from the German coast to at least ten miles west of Heligoland. These observations were made at 200 feet. The Commander-in-Chief required the squadron to mobilise at maximum strength for operation, night of 18th/19th February. A signal cancelled the operation.'

Jack Ramshaw had his DFM presented by AOC 3 Group Air Marshall Jackie Baldwin, whose belief in the bomber's ability to defend itself had proved so costly at the battle in which the DFM was won.

There was similar excitement elsewhere but stand-by was followed by stand-down the next night, then twenty Wellingtons did set off on the 20 February only to run into bad weather. There was fog at home and a recall signal was sent, too late for one crew of 38 Squadron who disappeared entirely. Another of 38 got lost and, after nine and a half hours in the air, ran out of petrol trying to find Marham. The crew abandoned ship and parachuted into Melton Constable, less than thirty miles from base. One of No. 99, force-landing in the prophesied fog, crashed into an orchard near Wisbech; no one killed.

If this was supposed to be the night-time equivalent of those daylight Heligoland raids it was also a complete failure. There would have been no fighter opposition but to bag three Wellington aircraft and six men, the Germans had not needed to do anything at all. They could leave it all to the misguided muddle-heads at the top of Bomber Command.

Most of the sea sweeping was handed to the Blenheims of 2 Group but the Wellingtons of 3 Group still went occasionally, and the Hampdens of 5 Group were learning their night-flying trade by nickelling.

Another type of training was 'Fighter co-operation', the RAF misnomer for exercises in non-co-operation with surrogate enemy fighters, and it was necessary practice because war was about to break out. Two of the veterans of Wilhelmshaven and North Coates Fitties would not live to see it. ORB, 9 Squadron, 8 March:

'Flying accident at Vickers Armstrong, Weybridge. Wellington 1A aircraft N3017 was returning to squadron after undergoing modification to fuel tank armour plating. Aircraft took off at 14.35 hours and was seen to crash shortly afterwards. The aircraft was totally destroyed by fire and all occupants were killed instantaneously. Court of Enquiry was held and found the accident to be due to an error of judgement.'

The occupants included the Canadian Flying Officer Bill Macrae DFC and his twenty-year-old observer from County Cork, Sergeant Cornelius Murphy.

Tragedy and comedy, like great wits and madness, can be divided by thin partitions and on 15 March a group of 77 Squadron Whitleys went on a leaflet raid, one of the few flown to Poland from France. The weather was fine on the way, but rain and a strong headwind were met on the long return journey. *The Times* reported the words of Flight Lieutenant B. Tomlin, one of the Whitley captains:

'We climbed to 18,000 feet above the clouds and judged by our instruments and ETA that we could not be very far from home. By this time my petrol gauge was showing nil, and I saw a hole in the clouds and came down.'

Thinking they were over France, Tomlin assumed that the single shell of anti-aircraft fire was just a warning. His opinion was confirmed when there was no more fire after he put his nav lights on and shot off the colours of the day:

'We landed in a field which sloped slightly ... and got out to meet the little group of peasants who were running towards us. I said "C'est la France, n'est-ce-pas?" One of them said "Non, non, Monsieur, c'est l'Allemagne – la frontière est à vingt kilometres," and pointed westward with a smile.
    'Like one man we turned and bolted for our machine. Other figures were hurrying towards us from the far end of the field. We started the engines in a flash and without pausing to thank anyone we got going.'

Shots were fired as they took off and they didn't come down again until they saw an advertisement for a popular French aperitif.

The French-speaking German peasant was a youth called Albert Kartes. He was arrested and accused of giving aid to the enemy but was released when the local constable was made to carry the can for failing to reach the enemy aircraft in time.

The seaplane bases on the Baltic islands of Sylt, Borkum and Nordeney had become a priority as they were a major source of mine laying off the UK coast. They were a legitimate target in that bombs could be dropped on the aircraft and on their 'runways' in the sea, but mainly the objective was harassment, to keep the seaplanes at home. It did work to an extent until the Germans modified land-based aircraft such as the He111 to do the mine laying.

Seventeen nights of ops by over seventy Whitleys saw bombs dropped three times, resulting in two bombs falling on Danish territory, Römö Island, and some more on the Sylt town of Westerland. This latter was not a concern as Sylt had been declared a fortified area by the Germans and so was deemed to have no civilians.

The ops were called 'security patrols' and in the freezing cold weather of that December and January, were monotonous and extremely uncomfortable for the crews. They continued through February, with Hampdens increasingly taking part, until mid-March when matters took a serious turn. German air attacks on the Royal Navy had had only modest success so far but, on the night of 17/18 March, five Heinkel 111s dive-bombed ships at Scapa Flow in the Orkney Islands. They damaged two, HMS *Norfolk* and HMS *Iron Duke*, killing four officers and wounding more. The rest of the formation went for an aerodrome nearby with insignificant results except that bombs fell on a tiny village, Bridge of Wraith, killing one civilian and wounding seven more.

The dead man, James Isbister, a council worker, had been standing in his doorway watching the action. The Germans claimed the civilian casualties were caused by detritus from British anti-aircraft fire. The British claimed that fifty bombs and many incendiaries had fallen on land wrecking several cottages, a car, and setting a farm building and straw stacks alight.

A gentlemanly response was devised – an attack on the seaplane base at Hörnum, at the far southern end of Sylt. It was a land target but, as stated, there were no civilians. Fifty bombers went – thirty Whitleys and twenty Hampdens – of 50, 51, 61, 102 and 144 Squadrons – with six hours allocated between them for their bombing runs over the base. Forty-one of the attackers claimed to have found the target in clear weather and to have hit it. Around twenty tons of general purpose bombs were dropped, plus 1,200 incendiaries, or about half a dozen Lancasters' worth, in the biggest job so far.

Intelligence officers were delighted to hear about the accurate bombing, although later reconnaissance showed little evidence of it. One Whitley was lost, shot down by flak. Canadian Flight Lieutenant John Baskerville and all his 51 Squadron crew were killed.

This was a first on many counts including baptism in war for many of the crews. It was also a technological first as the wireless operator in the leading aircraft was able to send coded messages reporting the attack, which started at 20.00, before it finished after 02.00, so that Mr Chamberlain could inform the House and the world that our bombers were hitting Germany while the raid was still going on – 'an event probably without precedent in the history of warfare' as *The Times* had it.

Another event that probably had plenty of precedents took place in Watford. Mrs Yvonne Reekie of Ivy Cottage, Bovingdon, went in her Rolls Royce to a grocer's shop and negotiated a price of two guineas while her chauffeur carried a hundredweight of sugar (112lb, about 50kg) in cardboard boxes to the car. They were spotted, reported and prosecuted. Mrs Reekie was fined £75 for obtaining the sugar ration of 120 people without a coupon.

Reconnaissance sorties, mostly by Blenheims, brought home information about navy and troops build-ups in German ports and various sailings north to what looked like jumping-off points for an invasion of Norway. In response, twenty-four Wellingtons of 9 and 115 Squadrons were moved to Lossiemouth on 2 April to form a bomber wing under the orders of Coastal Command.

The brief seemed to reverse recent trends. Although sea sweeps had been fairly frequent, training had concentrated on night flying. Now it looked as if they were back to Wilhelmshaven-style daylights, trying to bomb shipping. To get their hands in they did an exercise on 4 April. They had to change course several times and then search for a small island north-west of Orkney. They found it. Frank Petts:

> 'We were trained in night bombing of land targets, and we were being used in daylight against shipping. We'd been given postcard-size ship silhouettes with appropriate text,

something like "This is the *Hood*, one of ours", "This is the *Scharnhorst*, much the same size, attack on sight". Our means of attack was usually B bombs, which were like long, thin oil drums which weighed only 220lb and which, amazing to behold, floated.'

The idea was to fly just in front of the enemy warship at 10,000 feet or lower, and drop the B bomb so that when it bobbed back up to the surface said warship's thick armour plating would be obligingly steaming over it. Worried in case somebody more vulnerable might steam over, the bomb's designers had incorporated a humane self-sinking device. If the bomb for some hardly fathomable reason managed to miss the warship, the soap which held its nose-cone on would dissolve, the case would fill with water and down she would go. ORB, 9 Squadron:

'19 Naval Observers joined the wing for navigational duties. A few were trained Observers but the majority were sub-Lieutenants and Midshipmen inexperienced in air work.

'April 7th. The wing took off to attack a cruiser and six destroyers said to be 60 miles off the Danish coast. No contact was made. A listening watch was to be kept on 18 Group (Coastal Command) frequency but w/ops had to leave sets to load guns and man turrets so information was not reliably passed in the air.'

Frank Petts:

'One of our trips (7 April) was with six of 115 Squadron, to look for shipping off the Danish coast. We didn't find any but, on the way home, the 115 boys were jumped by a group of Me110s. It was over in an instant. Balch saw it, from the rear turret. "Fighters attacking behind ... they've got one of 115 ... he's on fire ... they're baling out ... they're shooting them up on the way down ... they've gone." You could argue that this was good practice. Shooting trained aircrew meant they couldn't come back at you again, assuming they might have survived the Danish sea in April without a dinghy.'

'Our (aeronautical) industry is so strong that we have not to import machines from abroad; we cannot use foreign machines as they are not good enough for our Luftwaffe.'

Flugsport, 10 April 1940.

German Airmen's Savagery
Wave of Bombers

'German bombers carried out a fresh wave of air raids over Norway during the week-end, states Reuter. The undefended coastal town of Aalesund, 150 miles north of Bergen, was subjected to a violent attack lasting more than two hours, says the Norwegian Telegraph Agency. Six machines crossed and recrossed the city dropping 500 lb explosive bombs. Many private houses were completely destroyed and a large number were made uninhabitable. People in the streets and a number of houses were attacked by machine-gun.'

The Times, 29 April 1940.

Balch saw one of two. N2949 KO/H, Pilot Office Roy Gayford and five crew, and P2524 KO/F, Canadian Pilot Officer Estelles Wickenkamp MBE, and five crew, are all commemorated at Runnymede.

Official reports again blamed the captains for not keeping in formation. Despite all the evidence, the high command still believed that self-defending bombers in close co-operation could defeat any fighter attack.

Britain had been becoming increasingly furious with neutral Norway. Thousands of tons of (neutral) Swedish iron ore were being shipped from the Norwegian port of Narvik to Germany and thence down the ship-canal system to the industrial heartland, the Ruhr. Britain's fury was thus a naval matter and the German navy was up there in strength too. The possibility of Britain invading Scandinavia had been put about by the German High Command for some time to divert attention from their own campaign of espionage, intrigue and fifth-column work aided by the notorious Vidkun Quisling. The Germans wanted Norway for themselves.

The Royal Navy laid mines inside Norwegian territorial waters in an attempt to stop the traffic. The Norwegian government issued a heated protest, threatening to declare war on Britain. The Allies jointly issued a list of sea areas into which Norwegian ships would sail at their peril.

The Germans were outraged, naturally. This was the most flagrant violation of neutrality ever seen. Added to which, the Allies were obviously too cowardly and weak to fight Germany directly, and so conducted an underhand war using the neutral countries as pawns in the game.

As the newspapers published the Allies' list of forbidden sea areas on the morning of 9 April, Germany simultaneously invaded Norway and Denmark. By the time British readers had moved on to the crossword and the latest advice from Lord Woolton to housewives, unresisting Denmark was occupied. The southern half of Norway followed after a stiff but short fight.

Such action was deeply regretted by Germany and it was only important military objectives that were the concern. It was all done to secure Scandinavia against Allied aggression. Germany would respect the freedom and independence of the peoples of Denmark and Norway and hoped very much that such respect would not be prejudiced by anything as silly as resistance, passive or active.

The Germans' real purpose was more complex than simply securing the iron ore. They did indeed want to prevent the Allies from setting up bases in Norway from which to attack northern Germany and they wanted naval bases – especially U-boat pens – and aerodromes to give them better access to their enemy's shipping lanes. Above all, they wanted to test just how determined and competent the Allies would be in a total war.

There was nothing the Allies could offer Denmark, but perhaps the Germans could be stopped in Norway. There wasn't really a strategy as such but clearly something had to be done. Soldiers would be landed at Narvik, too far north for the RAF to reach and offer support. Meanwhile, Bomber Command, without any fighter cover, was to slow the march of the Germans.

As the Aeronautical Correspondent of *The Times* put it, 'Command of the air over Norway will certainly have to be established before the Germans can be dislodged'. But the Luftwaffe had every important airbase in Norway and Denmark from which to operate, while every op for the RAF bombers had at least a 300-mile sea flight on either end of it. They were taking off from the UK mainland on the strength of scanty intelligence about a very fast-moving enemy who had caught everyone by surprise. The experience of 9 Squadron was typical. ORB:

> 'April 9th. Owing to invasion of Norway and Denmark, the squadron was allotted reconnaissance duties. In the morning, five sorties were flown and much enemy activity reported on sea, land and in the air.'

Reconnaissance duties were unallotted at 15.10, when orders were received to attack enemy cruisers at anchor in Bergen harbour. They took off at 15.40. The targets were located and bombs were dropped. No hits were observed by 9 Squadron, although others made claims, but Squadron Leader George Peacock did shoot down a Dornier Do18 flying boat. His immediate DFC was announced a few days later in the *London Gazette*:

> 'After the original attack by his formation he returned alone and repeated his run over the target in the face of heavy anti-aircraft fire. When on the return flight to his base he again turned back to attack a hostile flying-boat which was shot down into the sea.'

With two machine guns and a top speed of 150mph, the Dornier had little chance against the Wellington, once spotted. Its two diesel engines gave it excellent fuel economy and so a very long range, but it was very vulnerable in combat and was only in service because the Germans didn't have anything else yet. It would soon be relegated to air-sea rescue and training only.

The type is a double claimant to first German aircraft shot down by British aircraft in the Second World War. On 26 September 1939 Skuas of 803 Naval Air Squadron shot one up badly and forced it to 'land' in the sea, only for it to be blown apart by naval gunfire. This terrestrial second half of its demise may account for the rival claim of first blood by the crew of a 224 Squadron Lockheed Hudson who shot down another Dornier 18 off Jutland on 8 October 1939 with no third party involvement.

Next day, 10 April, Squadrons 9 and 115 were standing by at various levels of readiness, which were changed by the hour, until mid-afternoon when eleven Wellingtons of 9 and six of 115 took off to attack a large warship anchored off Kristiansund. They'd been in the air five minutes when the recall signal came from HQ.

The German troopship *Levante* was the target on 11 April for No. 9. Frank Petts remembered the briefing:

> 'Square McKee, our CO who was not coming on the op, asked us "Have the captains worked out how you are going to attack any German aircraft you see?" It seemed to be the unique preserve of sergeant pilots to get up the CO's nose, and I did it again by saying "Sir, we don't attack German aircraft. We run away from them." There followed a mild explosion and a dissertation on how easily a Wellington could dispose of German fighters. "Sir," I said, "how would you deal with one that sits back out of range of your guns and uses his cannon on you?" "Nonsense," said Square. "They can't do that."
>
> 'Well, I told him I knew from personal experience that they could, and they could also sit on top of you, where you can't get them but they can get you with their rear guns. "You're imagining things," said McKee. I suggested he asked Sergeant Ramshaw about imagination but McKee had the last word. He told us we'd never win the war with spirit like that. On the op our section split up, attacked by 110s. When we got back, the intelligence officers said there were no 110s so far north. I said my crew knew a 110 when they saw one, because we'd seen plenty at Wilhelmshaven.'

The 110s had already featured strongly in the invasion, which initially depended on paratroops taking and occupying key airfields and bridges. The troops were mostly in Ju52s and escorted by Me110s that would have twenty minutes' flying time left when they reached their targets, and so would circle while the paratroops took the airfields.

Things didn't quite go to plan, certainly not at Oslo-Fornebu, where a combination of orders mix-ups, errant Ju52s and Norwegian fighter pilots in Gloster Gladiators brought that part of the invasion to the very brink of disaster and caused Helmut Lent to crash-land his 110. But all went well for the Germans in the end.

The RAF was still not allowed to bomb Germany. All the ports where ships and troops had massed – and were still massing – could have been bombed but instead the bombers had to wait for the ships to set sail. An exception to the rule was military targets on mainland Norway occupied by the Germans. The prime one was Stavanger airfield. In the first raid of the war on a European land target, six Wellingtons of 115 were ordered to hit it; three did so. The other three didn't find it and one of those was shot down. Whether it was Me110s or the flak that got 115 Squadron's Wellington, we don't know, but the captain Pilot Officer Fred Barber and all his crew were killed in the crash.

Nothing at all is known about the other loss of that day, a 77 Squadron Whitley out from Driffield, part of a forty-plus effort of Hampdens and Whitleys on armed reconnaissance over the Skagerrak and Kattegat. A last wireless message was heard after seven and a half hours in the air, and that was all.

Back in Blighty the general opinion was that Hitler had gone a step too far. Norway, when reinforced by the Allies, would prove too tough. This was the feeling in 83 Squadron as they made ready for their first mine-laying trip. In the jargon, the mines were 'vegetables' and throughout the war the RAF 'planted' them in 'gardens', areas of sea with code names. In the Norway emergency with the new magnetic, allegedly unsweepable mines, the authorities had not yet got around to code names. Guy Gibson and colleagues were heading for the Great Belt, the *Store Bælt*, the central one of the three sea channels between Denmark and Norway/Sweden:

> 'We had to plant our mines at a dead reckoning position (11 April). After that we were to make a reconnaissance of Kiel harbour and check up on Middlefart (port of the Little Belt, the western channel) and the amount of activity going on there at the railway sidings. On no account were we to let our mines fall into the hands of the enemy.
>
> 'The trip itself was completely uneventful, and after eight hours we came home. In a Hampden the pilot can't move out of his seat, so after eight hours I was feeling pretty cramped, but worse was to come, nine, ten, eleven hours at a stretch. Two days later there was much excitement in the camp. Four

ships full of troops were reported to have been sunk with all hands near where we had been gardening.'

There was a major operation the following day, 12 April – in fact the biggest assault so far – with over eighty Wellingtons, Blenheims and Hampdens on a shipping attack at Stavanger. The Wimpy of 9 Squadron veteran of Brunsbüttel, Sergeant Charles Bowen, was one of ten aircraft lost – four Wellingtons and six Hampdens – four of them from 50 Squadron, to flak, to Me109s, to Me110s further north than they should have been. Only one of the ten had any surviving aircrew. German radio did admit the loss of five fighters.

Those bombers that came back reported ten-tenths cloud down to 600 feet, with horizontal visibility one mile in rain and sleet. This was the last time that Wellingtons and Hampdens were sent out in numbers in daylight. The core policy of pre-war strategists, that bombers could defend themselves while seeking their targets by day, was dumped at last, and would not be resurrected until the spring of 1944.

Another 50 Squadron Hampden was lost in the sea, possibly quite near the Lincolnshire coast, after being switched to gardening duties, early hours of 14 April, and later that day a much larger force of Hampdens, twenty-eight, set off to repeat the exercise. Guy Gibson was on this one with No. 83, a nine-hour flight to Little Belt and back, instrument flying almost all the way, forced so low by the cloud that, suddenly sighting Middlefart bridge right ahead he had no choice but to fly under it.

Three gardening Hampdens were lost, two without trace, one out of fuel trying to land on a beach in County Durham. And so it went on, small raids, gardening, aerodromes, losses every day and night and with the Germans not seemingly inconvenienced.

The advanced bomber wing of 9 and 115 Squadrons left Lossiemouth for their home bases on 14 April; No. 9 being one short of their original twelve and 115 two down. They would carry on, of course, taking the fight to the enemy while the great and the good concerned themselves with what the boys might be doing on leave. At a conference in London convened by the Lord Chamberlain, it was concluded that: 'Immediate steps should be taken to check the greater tendency which has become evident since the war at some places of entertainment, both in London and the Provinces, towards the giving of performances including nudity and impropriety of gesture and speech'.

The Germans' impropriety had brought them everything they wanted at very little expense. They were secure against attack through Scandinavia, they had ports like Bergen they could use for their U-boats against the American aid coming across the north Atlantic, they had fjords they could hide their battleships in, and they had their iron ore.

They had also humiliated the foe. They had invaded and taken two countries with the utmost speed and efficiency, meanwhile exposing the British and French as unable to do the slightest thing about it. There were hopeful articles in the press, small victories trumpeted and talk of a long campaign to reverse Hitler's great gamble, but the British and French governments were deeply shaken. If the Germans could conquer Poland, Norway and Denmark without any trouble at all, who was next?

A foreign correspondent of the *Scotsman* newspaper reported the official German view of Norway as a convenient air base from which to launch mass attacks on Britain. The Italian newspapers reported a visit to Rome by General Milch, Luftwaffe chief in Norway, when he said that Norway would be transformed into a great base for attack against England and that England was at the mercy of the German air force. The imminence of such attacks had already been announced in Berlin, while the Germans continued to accuse the Allies of bombing civilian targets and the Allies continued to deny it. The Supreme War Council meeting held in London on 27 April, which amounted to talks between the top air brass of UK and France, issued yet another denial, feeling sure that the German accusations were only a prelude to air raids in any case.

In between the two belligerents nervously sat the two neutrals, The Netherlands and Belgium. The Belgian foreign minister, Mr Spaak, said his country didn't want to be involved in other people's quarrels, and international law was the refuge of small nations. The British press pointed out that international law had not provided much of a refuge for Denmark and Norway.

The Dutch Prime Minister, Mr de Geer, said that neither France nor Germany need fear attacks by the other through Dutch territory because the defences of his country had been increased to the highest possible degree.

Meanwhile, Bomber Command concentrated entirely on Norwegian and Danish airfields, mine-laying and the seaplane bases. The aerodromes at Stavanger, Trondheim and Aalborg were attacked again and again, without much to show for it and with losses ticking up. Two Blenheims of 107 Squadron lost without trace on 17 April, Stavanger; one Wellington, 99 Squadron, likewise; one Whitley, 77 Squadron, Trondheim, ditched; another Wellington, 99 Squadron, Stavanger, in the sea; Whitley, 51 Squadron, Aalborg, lost without trace.

Many raids found little or nothing and suffered no losses either. Here is a typical example. The crews of six Wellingtons of 9 Squadron went on the night of 20/21 April to their first target on land, Stavanger aerodrome. They met bad weather over the target area. Frank Petts:

'We tried from several directions but southwards stretched a solid sheet of low stratus. We could not find a break although the last to arrive did and he was able to bomb. Gilbert Heathcote, whose father was a Brigadier General (and who would be killed in a Stirling at Brest in December 1941), had left my crew and was a skipper himself. He was coming back from this trip with not much idea of his position except it was over the sea somewhere, when the clouds suddenly broke and there were mountains smack in front. The crew never could agree afterwards on how much of a loop they did.'

For Stavanger, they'd taken off between 19.00 and 19.40 and returned over a period of four hours, first down 22.50, last 02.55, having dropped between them five 250lb bombs. They went to another aerodrome on the 24th, Westerland, on Sylt. Six took off, five found the target, three claimed to have hit it. Six went to Stavanger again on the 30th. They had six bombs each, five of which were delayed action for up to twelve hours. ORB:

'Each captain claims to have actually hit the aerodrome with the one bomb which was seen to burst. It is assumed that the remaining delayed action bombs were dropped on the aerodrome.'

In Brussels at the end of April 1940, the Belgo-Luxembourg section of the International Law Association proposed the creation of safe areas in every country, with no defences, no wireless stations and so on, where civilians could congregate and be secure from attack. All acts of hostility would be strictly forbidden and all States, whether belligerent or not, would sign up to the scheme.

Aircrew might have believed they'd had a hit but really they were doing well to get anywhere near their aiming points. Bomb aiming was not a specialised trade. In the bigger machines, the Whitleys and Wellingtons, the observer did it, leaving his navigator's table as the target approached to clamber into the nose, or the second pilot did it.

Still the arguments went on about bombing targets that were not strictly military. The British position seemed to be that so long as the Germans didn't bomb British civilians, the RAF would not attack Germans. That the Luftwaffe had already bombed Polish and Norwegian open cities, for example, did not come into the equation.

Lord Trenchard, founding father of the RAF, asked in Parliament what was meant by the Government's declaration about not bombing open towns. He pointed out that the Germans would happily bomb open towns as soon as such a stratagem suited them. Winston Churchill warned against exhausting our air force in Norway when there were other grave dangers.

As if to confirm his view, next day an RAF squadron of eighteen Gloster Gladiators, operating from a frozen Norwegian lake, was reduced to one serviceable aircraft by incessant Luftwaffe attacks. With the news that the Norwegian town of Kristiansund (population 15,000) had been burned to the ground after five days of bombing, the British Government reserved the right to withdraw orders prohibiting bombing civilian populations in the event of such bombing by the enemy.

They still didn't do it, though. It was more Norwegian airfields, more mine laying, more seaplanes, small numbers of attackers, not much damage.

For instance, McKee with George Peacock DFC as second pilot, led six Wellingtons of 9 Squadron for Rye aerodrome in central Denmark, about sixty miles inland from Arhus, while six more Wimpys plus twelve Whitleys were looking for Stavanger and Fornebu. ORB:

> 'The Danish coast was sighted at 21.15, approximately 5 miles south of Vorupor but an accurate pinpoint could not be made until Klitmonner was sighted (Klitmøller, 25 miles or so north). From here a course was set direct to Rye.'

This was a flight of about 230 miles, south-easterly, right across Jutland: 'The ETA at the target was 21.44 and although a search was made, Rye aerodrome could not be located.' Such an ETA must have been set at home before the flight. Surely such a gross miscalculation could not have been made in the air. It would be many years before bombers could do 500mph.

There were five of them by now; one had gone home with u/s gun turrets. They set off for the east coast and made a pinpoint at 55.45°N 10.05°E (probably Ashoved peninsula).

Here the formation separated, each aircraft setting a course from this point to Rye (now about 80 miles north-westerly). Two aircraft found the target and carried out attacks. The remaining aircraft searched the area for approximately one hour, between 1,500 and 8,000 feet, but were unable to find the target and therefore returned to base with full bomb loads.

The weather over Denmark was 'clear but hazy'. There was no opposition. The wind was not as forecast but even so, that was a very poor display, and a half-hearted one from the higher command. Five Wellingtons on a seven-and-a-half hour trip, wandering around Denmark so that a few bombs could be dropped severally from 1,500 feet and 10,000 feet. What was the point of it?

Whatever had been the preoccupations of the RAF, the British government, the press and everyone else during the last month, Norway and Denmark would be almost entirely forgotten soon after dawn on 10 May.

Preparations had been made in Bomber Command in case of an attack by the Germans through The Netherlands, Belgium and Luxembourg, amid many arguments with the French. The British wanted to attack the Ruhr with the heavy bombers, flying from England across the Low Countries in the expectation of destroying vital supplies of fuel and so on, which would greatly hinder the German advance.

The French didn't want that as it would set the Luftwaffe free to bomb French cities and the British bombers' effects on the Ruhr would not be felt in the short term. They urged battle-support from the heavies, and from the France-based Blenheims and Battles. Air Marshal Portal, Commander-in-Chief of Bomber Command, was certain that fifty Blenheims and a hundred Battles would be able to do little to stop the Wehrmacht and would suffer huge losses in the process. Although it had been shown in several conflicts that bombers could be useful in support of an advancing army, there was no history of bombers trying to stop one.

CHAPTER 6

Blitzkrieg

Mick Maguire, in France with 88 Squadron:

'We all knew it was coming. We'd been getting constant high-flying Dorniers and Junkers 88s coming over, obviously taking photographs. There'd even been one published in the *Illustrated London News* and we had a copy, captioned saying this was supposed to be a British airfield in France. Supposed to be? It was, it was our airfield, and I took it to show our CO who was ex Royal Flying Corps and in France for the second time. He said to send our warrant officer to see him, which then was Dizzy Dickson, ex infantry from the first war. When he came back he went straight up to me and said "CO's seen the photograph and says shift the bomb dump".

'Our field-kitchen chap, who made the best bacon sandwiches in France, had already moved. He'd taken all his stuff from outside the main hangar to as far from it as possible, which he did a fortnight before the blitz started. Three or four miles away was the barn we slept in, which is where we were when the first bombs fell on the first morning of the blitzkrieg. We jumped on our bikes and pedalled as fast as we could to find that it hadn't been our airfield that was bombed.'

The British high command must also have known it was coming unless they entirely disbelieved the evidence of their own aircraft going over and taking photographs. The Germans hadn't depleted

their western air force presence by much for the Norway invasion.
Now the aerodromes in the west were becoming highly populated.
Armoured columns were camped on the borders. Troops and war
materiel were massing and were clear and obvious targets for bombing and strafing, but none was done. Some civilians might have been
hit. The French feared aerial reprisals. So the Germans continued
their preparations undisturbed.

As news came through of the German invasion of The Netherlands
on Friday 10 May, 40 Squadron was ordered to send a small formation
of Blenheims to find out what was happening. There were, it was
reported, German paratroops on the main airfields. Blenheims of
18 Squadron based at Méharicourt in France had similar orders and
all took off soon after 09.00.

Pilot Officer Geoffrey Harding, twenty-one, and his observer Sergeant
Kenneth Shrosbree, of 18 Squadron were probably the first Bomber
Command casualties of that dreadful day, but two Blenheims of
40 Squadron, based in England at Wyton, cannot have been far
behind. One crew was taken prisoner; the other, after being shot up
by a Ju88, made it home to add to the squadron's news sufficient for
a raid to be organised on Ypenburg aerodrome, near The Hague.

There was only one surviving crew member out of the three
Blenheims lost at Ypenburg and while other Blenheims of 57 and
18 Squadrons went down, the Battles of the AASF had been waiting
for the signal to fly at the enemy. As the Luftwaffe bombed and
strafed targets in France, all Allied bombers had been grounded on
the orders of the French Commander-in-Chief General Gamelin who
clung with supreme obstinacy to the hope that a 'bombing war' could
somehow be avoided. Air Marshal Sir Arthur 'Ugly' Barratt, AOC of
the RAF in France, took the decision himself and sent in the Battles.

Their target was a column of German troops reported by a French
reconnaissance aircraft some hours earlier as advancing through
Luxembourg. There was no fighter escort available; the four squadrons
of Hurricanes now in France were supremely busy trying to repel
wave after wave of Luftwaffe bombers.

Orders for the Battles were to go in very low and drop bombs fused
for eleven seconds' delay. They did as ordered and met furious anti-
aircraft fire from the ground including machine guns and small arms,
and three Battles fell straight away.

At Mourmelon, there was no word yet. Maguire:

'There didn't seem to be much in the way of orders about what to do. The French were still being difficult about us flying independently of them in their country, so we were lounging about, lying on the grass near the hangar when a flight of Blenheims went over, recognisable from their duck-egg blue undersides. One of our number remarked on this and I said "I've got news for you. They're Junkers 88s", and as I said it they peeled off and side slipped down to attack us. We ran like hell and they did our hangar completely.'

Two Fairey Battles were destroyed in that attack before they could get into the air. Among those who did make contact with the enemy, 12 Squadron lost four with, amazingly, nobody killed. Three went down from 103, four from 105, again with no fatalities, four from 142, three men dead, four from 150, one of 218 and two of 226.

That made a total of twenty-four Battles lost or damaged beyond repair in the first hours of the new, non-phoney war, plus ten Blenheims making thirty-four aircraft by the end of the day. Fighter Command had had losses too. For example, five out of six of their Blenheims attacking Waalhaven aerodrome were shot down by a flock of Me110s.

There was a new prime minister at the end of that day, Winston Churchill, and British troops crossed the Belgian border from France to meet the Germans. Also on this day, some Luftwaffe Heinkel He111s got lost on their way to a French target and bombed one of their own cities – Freiburg – by mistake, killing about sixty people. In the heat of all the blitzkrieg success and excitement, as the German army and air force began their bash through Western Europe, Hitler still found time to charge the British with the inhuman cruelty of bombing the innocent citizens of Freiburg.

As evening came, nine Whitleys of 77 and 102 Squadrons left Driffield for targets in Germany. They were aiming for bridges across the Rhine and mechanised columns of troops between the border and the Rhine. This was the first time that RAF bombers had attacked the German mainland – nine of them, at night, trying to hit bridges. The troops would have been easier – they'd have had their lights on –

and 77 Squadron did claim to have attacked a column of lorries. The effect on the blitzkrieg was not noticeable.

On the same night, thirty-six Wellingtons set off to attack Waalhaven aerodrome, near Rotterdam. In one was a new boy, second pilot Sergeant Rupert 'Tiny' Cooling, twenty years old, the tallest man in the squadron and just arrived from training school:

'The phoney war was over and everywhere was bustle and confusion. The spectre of 18 December hovered over the airfield (Honington) and for us freshmen, thrown together with some experienced fellows and told that we were now a crew, it was bewildering and ominous. After a few false starts we eventually had a briefing. We were to crater Waalhaven airfield and soften up the German army there, in support of a Dutch counter attack.

'Navigator Sgt Jock Gilmour worked out his course and captain Sgt Douglas decided to stay low over the sea, climb on seeing the coast, and make a bombing run east to west in line with the route home.

'As we climbed above the shore, the setting sun glinted on windows and narrow waterways, and up ahead there was another set of lights, in a curtain, rising from the ground with smoke behind. It was my job to shut the wireless operator into the front turret, then I was ordered into the astrodome to watch for fighters although we weren't really expecting any. As we went into our bombing run routine, the curtain of lights was dead ahead, rising balls of pink, green, white, slowly ascending towards us then hurtling past. Then three things happened at once. The flak curtain seemed to part and let us through, there was the bucking bronco effect of dropping our bombs, and I heard a smacking sound like hands clapping. I looked, and we had a hole in our wing. "Pilot from second pilot," I said. "We've been hit outboard of the starboard engine." I was quite surprised to hear myself on the intercom. I sounded rather nonchalant.'

Cooling flew the aircraft over the sea while Douglas checked the damage – the damage that he could see, that was:

'The skipper took over for the landing, and we were down, and then we tugged viciously to the right and ended up square across the flarepath. The flak had punctured our starboard tyre, we had a self-sealing fuel tank bulging out like a huge hæmorrhoid dripping and ready to burst, and we had holes punctured all over the starboard engine. After the interrogation, where they gave you sweet milky tea and as many cigarettes as you could smoke, Sgt Douglas bought me a pint. So, that was it. My first trip. It was good to be home. And I'd learned that it was possible to go out and come back.'

Everyone else was home too and reported to the intelligence officer: 'All bombs were dropped and every captain claims to have dropped them on the aerodrome.'

By dawn on the 11th, it was clear that one of the main German thrusts was through Maastricht towards Brussels. Blenheims of 18 Squadron were sent to recce; two were lost. Pre-empting any more such missions, the Luftwaffe bombed airfields at Condé-Vraux and Ecury-sur-Coole, destroying seven Blenheims on the ground belonging to 114 and 150 Squadrons. The attackers were nine Do17s. They had hedge-hopped all the way from Aschaffenburg in Bavaria and crossed the Maginot Line before anyone woke up to what was happening. They found the Blenheims fuelled and bombed up, ready to fly on ops. *The Luftwaffe War Diaries*:

'That the Blenheims happened to be lined up as if on parade was a coincidence that no-one had reckoned with. The German bombers could scarcely miss. Their 100lb bombs fell in regular lines right among them.'

The squadron was almost destroyed. Two more Blenheims of 110 Squadron were shot down attempting a strike at Maastricht from Wattisham. Four Battles of 218 were detailed to attack a German column on the Belgian-German border; all four were shot out of the sky. Four Battles of 88 Squadron had a similar task and, like the 218 boys, didn't get a proper chance to do their work.

The four were aiming north for Bouillon, on the French/Belgian border. Pilot Officer Norman Riddell, whose father served with

88 Squadron RFC, came in with an irreparable Battle at No. 1 Squadron's Hurricane base at Vassincourt, near Bar-le-Duc, about fifty miles to the east of Mourmelon. Flight Lieutenant Madge and his w/opAG Corporal Collyer were taken prisoner near the target; observer Sergeant Edward Whittle was killed. Pilot Officer Mungovan and observer Sergeant Robson also became POWs while nineteen-year-old Aircraftman First Class Eric Maltby died fifty miles the other side of the target, at St Vith on the Belgian/German border. Nearby was the only total loss for 88 Squadron that day, Pilot Officer Bruce Skidmore aged twenty, Sergeant Ronald Kirby and Aircraftman First Class William Parsons – all for Hotton War Cemetery.

The night began with yet another Blenheim shot down, an 18 Squadron machine on a recce, all crew killed, but the main event was the first bombing raid on a German town. Even so, the target could not be the town itself, but rather the roads and railways leaving it, the so-called exits of München Gladbach. Hampdens and Whitleys of 49, 77, 144 and other squadrons, a force of less than forty aircraft altogether, left England at various times. Most of them reached the target but very little damage was done except to the invaders who lost three machines. Four men were killed and one taken prisoner in a 77 Squadron Whitley, while a Hampden of 144, severely damaged by flak, was steered as far as the Maginot Line by its pilot, Wing Commander Arthur Luxmoore, who ordered his crew out but was himself killed when he eventually crashed in southern Belgium.

Those that returned reported tremendous troop movements, continuous streams of vehicles, headlights blazing and rumbling along the roads from east to west. Next day, the third day of the blitzkrieg would prove to be the blackest yet for Bomber Command. This was a full-scale test of what bombers could do when trying to halt an advancing army.

First in the air were the Blenheims of 139 Squadron, nine of them setting off at dawn to bomb columns of troops leaving Maastricht – where the major bridges over the Albert Canal had been secured – and heading south into Belgium. The bombers found their target at more or less the same time as a swarm of Me109s found them. The fight was over in the blinking of an eye. *The Luftwaffe War Diaries*:

'A hundred yards astern of the last of them, Adolph (Lt Walter Adolph, formation leader of 2 Staffel, I/JG1) went down, then coming up again approached obliquely from below. The bombers stuck rigidly to their course. Hadn't they noticed anything? In his reflector sight, the Blenheim appeared as big as a haystack.'

At eighty yards the Blenheim had no chance against combined cannon and machine-gun fire. Within five minutes Adolph shot down two more. Three other pilots claimed one each. As the last three bombers tried to escape they were spotted by another *Staffel* of Me109s near Liège and they claimed two.

Only one of the Blenheims is known to have gone down there. Squadron Leader Tideman and Sergeant Hale were able to make their way on foot back to France. Leading Aircraftman John Rooney, age twenty, was killed.

Among the other fourteen dead and the wreckage of seven Blenheims lay the body of Flying Officer Andrew McPherson DFC, he who had flown the first mission of all on 3 September and who now died in the same aircraft, N6215.

Next up were the Battles of 12 Squadron; their targets were two of the Albert Canal bridges. The day before, nine Belgian Battles had tried it and lost six.

Volunteers were asked for. Every pilot wanted to go, so the CO elected the next six crews on the duty roster. Flying Officer Garland was to lead his section to attack the metal bridge at Veldwezelt while Flying Officer Thomas led his to the concrete bridge at Vroenhoven. The two leaders disagreed about how the job should be done. Thomas was intending to dive bomb his bridge while Garland was going in at zero feet.

One of Thomas's crews found their machine u/s, so jumped into another, to find that u/s too. There were no more, so Thomas set off with just Pilot Officer Davey and crew. The flak and the fighters were too much for them but the result was nobody killed, four POWs, two men safe in France, two Fairey Battles wrecked entirely and a little damage on and around the bridge.

Garland's section went in at low level, line astern. The flak got hotter and hotter and soon Pilot Officer McIntosh's machine was hit in the main petrol tank and immediately became, as Maguire put it, a flying fire hazard. In flames and with bombs jettisoned, the Battle crashed not far away. The crew struggled out and hid, but were soon found. One of their captors told them what fools they were:

> 'You British are mad. We capture the bridge early Friday morning. You give us all Friday and Saturday to get our flak guns up in circles all around the bridge, and then on Sunday, when all is ready, you come along with three aircraft and try and blow the thing up.'

By that time the raid was over. Part of the bridge was down which meant the Germans had to go around by another bridge, and the other two Battles were burning on the ground with all men dead.

Donald Garland and his observer, Sergeant Thomas Gray, were posthumously awarded the Victoria Cross, the first such for the RAF in the Second World War. To the eternal disgrace of whoever decides these things, the w/opAG, Leading Aircraftman Lawrence Royston Reynolds, age twenty, was not recognised at all for his part in the attack although he was just as dead.

The Garlands were a very loyal family. Father Patrick was awarded the CMG for services to Empire and Donald's three brothers, Patrick, John and Desmond, all died in service with the RAF in that war.

Desperate air strikes filled the rest of the day, 12 May, with similar outcomes. Troops advancing through eastern Belgium near Bouillon were dive-bombed by 103 and 218 squadrons. They lost four Battles at Neufchâteau; 150 lost two. At St Hubert, 105 lost two. It seemed to aircrew that you had a fifty-fifty chance of survival, which is to say a life expectancy of two ops.

As the day ended, the 135 serviceable aircraft of Bomber Command based in France on 10 May had become seventy-two, but that wasn't all. Coming over from England with the same brief, 107 Squadron lost four Blenheims and 15 Squadron lost seven, which made thirty-four Bomber Command losses on the day.

Of course, Bomber Command also had many more serviceable aircraft in the UK, but it is instructive to see how many the Germans had, waiting to pounce from their forward positions in support of the blitzkrieg. *The Luftwaffe War Diaries* gives these numbers:

> Bombers – Do17, He111, Ju88 – 1,120
> Dive-bombers – Ju87 (Stuka), Hs123 – 366
> Fighters – Me109, Me110 – 1,264

One of two Battles down at Vroenhoven, 12 May 1940 – P2332 PH/F of 12 Squadron, flown by F/O Norman Thomas. He and his crew were taken prisoner.

That night of 12 May, six Wimpys and six Whitleys tried to find road junctions, hoping to slow movements from the Rhine to The Netherlands, while there were several new diners in the officers' mess at Honington, one of whom already was very unusual indeed, and another who would be so.

Sedgwick Whiteley Webster, known as Bill, of Litchfield County, Connecticut, was born in South Africa of American parents in 1904. At his age, he was *hors de combat*. The army certainly wouldn't have him, or the navy, but the RAF seems to have been old fashioned enough to be able to find a place for an American gentleman who simply wanted to help.

If being a US citizen in RAF Bomber Command was not enough to make him unique at that moment, his other qualifications certainly were. He was new aircrew yet positively ancient. He was not some young daredevil pilot wanting to climb into a Spitfire. They made him an air gunner, probably to give him something to do since he'd so kindly volunteered to fight and it was a short training course. They made him an officer, only Pilot Officer, the lowest rank, the equivalent of army lieutenant, but officer nevertheless.

As we have noted, air gunning then was not really considered a separate skilled trade. Gunners were wireless operators, w/opAGs, who manned the guns when they needed to, or they could be pretty well anybody who would fill in.

Webster thus was one of the first designated gunner-only aircrew who had not been wireless trained, and one of the first, if not the first, wartime volunteer of officer rank in that job. Most w/opAGs were aircraftman grades, although some of the longer serving regulars had reached as high as sergeant. Bill Webster was all this, and an American, and he was destined to become more unusual still.

Webster was posted from 214 training squadron with his pilot pal Bertram 'Jimmy' James (all those with the surname James were likely to be nicknamed Jimmy, after the much loved comedian of the time). They would very soon be crewed up with B-flight commander Squadron Leader Peacock DFC, an officer with long service in Empire policing and an acknowledged brilliant pilot. James would be second pilot with Webster in the rear turret. Jimmy James:

> 'Bill was ten years and more older than the rest of us so he was the old man of the crew, a nice, friendly fellow whom we held in great respect.'

R.A.F TRIUMPH IN 'TOTAL WAR'
150 Enemy Machines Shot Down

'Germany has paid a high price for her air attacks on France and the Low Countries. In three days of "total war" it is estimated that they have lost something like 150 machines to R.A.F. squadrons stationed in France. As is only to be expected, we have also suffered losses, but they are only a fraction of those of the enemy.'

The Times, 13 May.

INTENSIVE AIR FIGHTING

'A pilot officer of the R.A.F Fighter Command had an anxious few minutes near Rotterdam early yesterday morning when, after shooting down a Junkers 87 bomber in flames and attacking three more Junkers, he found that he had joined formation by mistake with two Messerschmitt 109 fighters. As he had used up all his ammunition he climbed into cloud and returned to his base.'

The Times, 14 May.

Three years hence, James would find his description posted all over Germany and the Occupied Countries and broadcast over national radio as part of a *Grossfahndung* (national alert):

'JAMES Bertram Arthur. Born 17.4.1915 in Assam, India. Height: 170 cms. Dark brown hair, oval face, blue grey eyes, small narrow nose. Has all his teeth. Small figure. Healthy complexion.'

The eye colour, the Gestapo might have noted later, was actually brown. James and three other 9 Squadron pilots from this time, Tom Kirby-Green, 'Conk' Canton, and Les Bull, would reconvene in POW camp, Stalag Luft III.

Nothing much happened on the 13th in Bomber Command. There was a small op by Battles of 226 Squadron aimed at the roads near Breda. A hit was claimed on a crossing and one Battle went down with nobody killed. If it was a day for licking wounds and taking stock, the news from the Front made tomorrow look like the biggest day yet. The Germans had reached the River Meuse near Sedan in a spearhead attack, while the French 9th Army had obligingly vacated the Sedan area and moved north to confront the Germans in Belgium. The Luftwaffe had flown 500 bombing sorties in the late afternoon, well in front of their ground forces, keeping the French artillery quiet and stopping any attempts at reinforcement. Huge numbers of German reinforcements could be seen moving unhindered to support the spearhead and their 1st Rifle Regiment was over the river.

Any cold analysis would have made the situation hopeless, but retreat was not yet an option. In the early morning of 14 May, ten Battles of 103 and 150 Squadrons attacked German pontoon bridges in the Sedan area and suffered no losses. These squadrons would be flying again later, with altogether different results.

The French attacked around the middle of the day and in one hour of the afternoon, between 15.00 and 16.00, every available Battle was sent, with the last functioning French-based Blenheim squadron, No. 139, against the Sedan bridgehead. It was named 'the day of the fighters' by the German Air Corps, but it was the day of the flak gunners too if all the figures were to be believed. The fighters flew over 800 sorties and claimed 179 Allied aircraft shot down. The gunners claimed another 112. Not counting the many French losses, and the

British Hurricanes also downed, the AASF Battle squadrons suffered thus: 12 Squadron lost four aircraft; 88 Squadron two; 103 Squadron (for some reason flying with crews of just two men) three; 105 Squadron seven; 139 Squadron, four Blenheims; 142 Squadron, four Battles; 150 Squadron, four; 218 Squadron, five; 226 Squadron, four.

In the evening 2 Group sent more Blenheims over from England and 21 Squadron lost three, 110 Squadron five, 114 Squadron one. The total for the day was forty-seven, almost exactly half of the sorties flown. No such losses had ever been imagined, much less seen before, nor would a proportion like that occur again in a sizeable operation – but then, never again would such an imbalance be struck between huge numbers of modern fighters against so many unsuitable, vulnerable bombers.

'In the fury of these engagements (at Sedan) detailed reports from aircraft crews cannot be expected. Heavy losses must be suffered in attacking vital objectives which are strongly defended by anti-aircraft fire and enemy fighters. Our losses, which are not considered excessive in view of the results obtained, were 35 aircraft. Several crews from these aircraft, however, have already returned to their aerodromes.'

Air Ministry statement, 15 May.

CHAPTER 7

Gloves Off

Elsewhere on 14 May events even more significant for the bomber war were unfolding. Rotterdam was strongly garrisoned and the officer commanding, Colonel Scharroo, saw no reason to capitulate to German forces that he knew would take a severe battering were they to attempt to take the city. Negotiations during a ceasefire did not progress.

A formation of 100 Heinkel 111s was ready to bomb the city into surrender and the Germans were using this aerial bombardment as a threat. What neither side knew, according to German sources, was that while talks went on between Scharroo and his German counterpart, General Schmidt, the bombers were on their way and that signals to hold them back had failed to reach them. Hundreds of red Very lights, the agreed 'abort' signal, went unnoticed by the bombers, which proceeded to smash the old centre of Rotterdam into smithereens and start fires that could not be put out.

The Germans said that Rotterdam's fire brigade was to blame for not having modern equipment, and all those margarine and cooking oil warehouses had fuelled the flames. Had it not been for errors in wireless transmission and the invisibility of a mass display of red Very lights, the bombs would not have been dropped and 800 of the ordinary folk of Rotterdam would not have been killed.

So, we have to ask, what would the Germans have done if the wireless messages and so on had recalled the bombers, while Colonel Scharroo had remained adamant as, militarily speaking, he surely would have? Perhaps the Heinkels would have been debombed and the crews given a week's leave. Perhaps the German army would have ignored Hitler's orders to subdue The Netherlands in short order, camped in the Rotterdam suburbs and made friends with the natives.

In any case, much to the horror of the rest of the world, Germany bombed an open city and killed a great many non-combatants, as surely was intended. The Dutch surrendered the next morning, thus providing the Germans with the Hiroshima Opening: a great many more people, including soldiers of both sides, were saved by the Rotterdam air raid who would otherwise have perished had the fighting continued through the streets.

Whatever the truth of the matter, the old restrictions on bombing had been consigned to history. The task for which Bomber Command had been formed could now be tackled.

On 15 May several important things happened. The British butter ration was halved to 4oz per person per week, sugar from 12oz to 8oz, Rommel smashed up the French tank regiments and full authority to bomb Germany was given to the RAF at last.

They opened with ninety-nine aircraft, Wellingtons, Hampdens and Whitleys, to sixteen targets in the Ruhr. These were highly particular aiming points – war-effort factories, refineries, railways and power stations – with specific flights of bombers assigned to each. For instance, six Whitleys of 58 Squadron were sent to the marshalling yards at Wanne-Eickel (now Herne), and six of 115 to a factory in Duisburg. Three of the targets were considered especially important and were allotted nine bombers. Every crew had an alternative should the primary not be reached and seen.

Skippers were given their targets, the weather forecast and information about the opposition they might meet. There were virtually no night-fighters at this time but most of the crews had yet to experience the concentrations of searchlights and flak they would find tonight. Those who had been on nickelling raids were used to flying high, above the flak. Now they would have to go in much lower, 10,000 feet or less, if they were going to have a chance of seeing their objectives.

General take-off times were briefed and a point given at which to cross the English coast but after that it was up to the skippers and navigators, who worked out the rest of their routes and how they would attack. Here's Guy Gibson writing about a raid a few days later:

'As Jackie (Withers, observer) and I wanted to get to a movie at Lincoln that night, we decided to take off late. Our plan was to attack at between three and four in the morning. We reckoned it would be getting light then and the glow in the north, coupled with the light of the moon, would make target identification very easy.'

These crews were greatly optimistic and immensely enthusiastic. They did not doubt that they would be able to drop their bombs right down that factory chimney.

Realistically, they had no chance of doing such a thing and it was quite ridiculous (with hindsight) for the top brass to expect it. In cloud or fog, which invariably seemed to cover the Ruhr, and with no possibility of matching the terrain below to the map on his table, the navigator had to work on dead reckoning. A side wind could easily knock an aircraft ten miles off track, or fifty for that matter. With experience, ambition would be reeled in: get within twenty miles or so of the target and scout around for some confirming landmarks (which, of course, would not be there if the aircraft was too far away). In any case, if you imagine Sheffield and Rotherham joined together and multiplied ten times into a smoky industrial sprawl, how do you tell one steelworks from another at 10,000 feet, even if you could see them properly?

On this night, the first of many, there was nobody with such experience. As an example, we shall follow the six Wellingtons of No. 9 Squadron aiming for Bottrop, the German coal-mining equivalent of Barnsley, taking off at irregular intervals between 20.50 and 22.35 to look for the giant coke-processing works. ORB:

'At between 5,000 and 11,000 feet, the first four aircraft found a cloudless sky (over the target area) but very hazy. The last two aircraft arriving at approximately 00.45 and 01.15 encountered eight tenths cloud at 10,000 feet.'

If any bombs fell on Bottrop that night, there is no record of it. On the way home, the squadron's individuals flew through powerful electrical storms which rendered wireless sets u/s. One crash landed near Epping. While the only casualty of the night, a Wellington

OPERATIONS RECORD BOOK.

DETAIL OF WORK CARRIED OUT.

By No. 9 Squadron.

From 2050hrs. 15 / 5 / 40 to 0320hrs. 16 / 5 / 40

Aircraft Type and No.	Crew	Duty	Time Up.	Time Down.	Details of Sortie or Flight.	References.
Wellington L. 7795.	S/L. MONYPENNY. P/O. MAUDE-ROXBY. SGT. WATSON. SGT. COWELL. P/O. LEES. SGT. COOK.		2050	0200	In accordance with H.Q. No. 3 Group instructions, form B.135, dated 15th May, 1940, six aircraft of No. 9 Squadron carried out a raid against target A. 69. Aircraft proceeded singly, taking off at irregular intervals between 2050 and 2235 hours. On the route out between the English and Dutch	
L. 7796.	SGT. DOUGLAS. SGT. COOLING. SGT. GILMOUR. SGT. OLIVER. SGT. HORRY. SGT. WILLIAMS.		21.05	0110	coastay weather was hazy up to 5,000 feet. Above that it was fairly clear. Between the Dutch coast and target, clouds gradually formed varying between 2/10ths and 8/10ths., between 5,000 and 11,000 feet. Over the target area, the first four aircraft found a cloudless sky, but very hazy. The last two air-	
P. 9278.	SGT. KITSON. SGT. LAWSON. SGT. ROSEKILLY. SGT. WHITHAM. SGT. PARKER. SGT. READ.		2110	0140	craft, arriving at approximately 00.45 to 01.15 hours, encountered 8/10ths. cloud at 10,000 feet. Due to thick haze and clouds, the target was very difficult to locate. Four aircraft encountered a violent thunderstorm between the Dutch and English coasts on the route	
P. 9231.	F/LT. RIVETT-CARNAC. P/O. WANKLYN. SGT. JONES. SGT. SMITH. P/O. ASHTON. SGT. CROUCH.		2130	0225	home. One aircraft DCF. 179, was badly struck three times by lightning, causing a valve to be fused in the wireless set, also terrific sparks shot off from the leading edge of the main planes, airscrews and front turret of the aircraft. The other three aircraft complained of receiving brush discharge	

No. of pages used for day...........

Here is recorded one small part of the first permitted air raid on mainland Germany. The target was the coke works at Bottrop, in the Ruhr, which was not hit, and the journey home was nearly a disaster.

Aircraft Type and No.	Crew.	Duty.	Time Up.	Time Down.	Details of Sortie or Flight.	References.
Wellington L. 7788.	P/O. WALSH. SGT. CANTON. SGT. BRUCE. SGT. COSTAIN. P/O. VAUGHAN. SGT. COOPER.		2210	0310	of a less violent nature. The wireless sets in the aircraft of FOF. 175, LOF. 177 and DOF. 179 were put out of action by the electrical storms. Due to this, two aircraft were unable to definitely locate themselves. FOF. 175 made a forced landing at SHOREHAM, and LOF. 177 made a forced landing on	
P. 9239.	SGT. BULL. SGT. BROOKS. SGT. BETTS. SGT. GANNON. SGT. PETERS. SGT. DOBSON.		2230	0320	a dummy flare path at NAZEING, near EPPING. IN connection with this forced landing the Captain states that at the time he was flying in heavy rain, and as the W/T. set was unserviceable, he could not locate his position. On locating this dummy flare path, and after circling round several times, he decided to land, as he thought it was an aerodrome. He also states that he signalled several times, but received no signal from the ground, which is correct for a dummy flare path. High level bombing was carried out by all aircraft between 9,000 and 12,000 feet. Two Captains considered that they had bombed the correct target. The other four Captains were unable to locate the primary target, and therefore carried out attacks on what they considered was the secondary target A.367. Intense searchlight activity was encountered, but A.A. fire, which was fairly plentiful, was inaccurate. There was no opposition from enemy fighters.	
					LOF. 177, which made a forced landing was severely damaged, but on a dummy flarepath at NAZEING, near EPPING. The crew were unhurt.	

of 115 Squadron, got entirely lost and crashed in France, killing all the crew, some of No. 9 were cruising unknowingly up and down the English south coast, setting off the air raid sirens in Hastings. Tiny Cooling:

> 'We got to the Ruhr all right. God knows if we got to Bottrop. We saw St Elmo's Fire for the first time, which turned the props into blue disks and there was a flickering lilac rainbow arc between the two front guns. Our wireless had gone for a loop and Dougie (Sgt Douglas, captain) said the compass was drifting idly around and around, and we flew along with absolutely no idea of where we were or where we might be going. It was a kind of limbo, eerie really, and then somebody said "Maybe we're over England", so we came down through the cloud and saw we were over land but we didn't know which land. We signalled SOS with the downward recognition light and a flarepath lit up. Of course, the Germans knew SOS as well as we did, and I was standing by with the Very pistol ready to fire the aircraft. But it was the strip of a private aero club at Shoreham-by-Sea which, like a lot of south coast landing fields, had been alerted because of the expected escape of the Belgian royal family, following the Dutch a few days before. We weren't quite that important so we were offered sofas and chairs to kip down on in the flying club.
>
> 'I don't know if our w/op Sgt Oliver had been practising his French in Morse or if he was perfecting his knowledge of Q codes*. Maybe nobody had told him that we were landing. Anyway, he hadn't wound in his trailing aerial and we lost it on the roof of Lancing College. They rang up next day and said they'd got sixty feet of copper wire with some lead balls on the end and did it belong to us. So Oliver was in for a half-crown fine for losing his aerial.'

* Q codes were Morse abbreviations: QAA – airborne at (hrs); QBG – I am above cloud; QBH – I am below cloud; QBF – I am in cloud or, more popularly, I am a bloody fool; etc. Q code plus IMI became interrogative: QAH IMI – what is your height? Many w/ops prided themselves on their encyclopaedic knowledge and lightning use of Q codes.

This should get us home all right, chaps. The British Standard aerodrome radio location beacon of 1939/40 could easily have been copied by any child with a Meccano set.

Douglas was first down that night, 01.10. Sergeant Les Bull, one destined for Stalag Luft III and the Great Escape, didn't get home until 03.20.

Whoever wrote the copy for this 1939 advertisement could not have fully understood the awful truth of the words. A 'necessity during flights the duration of which approximates the range of the aircraft,' indeed.

BRITISH BOMBERS' SUPERIORITY

'The loads which British night bombers can carry are much greater than the loads which German bombers can carry. This is of some importance, as it has been found that it is of value to be able to use bombs of large size in salvoes for certain kinds of target. Larger numbers of machines carrying smaller loads cannot therefore be as effective.'

The Times Aeronautical Correspondent, 17 May.

'We had an exercise in what to do when the Germans raided us. My husband was appointed Chief Air Raid Warden, and I was ambulance driver. The ambulance was our van that we used on the farm. The schoolmaster's wife was in the Red Cross so she was in charge of the nurses in the village hall. Casualties were villagers with a label saying what their supposed injuries were. The schoolmaster's wife read one out. "Broken hip. Right, first thing, remove his trousers." Whereupon the air-raid victim leapt from his stretcher and ran out of the hall.'

Mrs Mary Hovells, School Farm,
Ilketshall St Lawrence, Suffolk.

Another two half-dozens of bombers attacked roads and railways in Belgium on the same night without loss so that meant 111 aircraft went and 110, one way or another, came back eventually, some with flak damage but nothing too serious. This was easily the biggest venture so far and it had not proved costly – which was just as well, as it hadn't achieved anything either. A bomb fell on a farm near Cologne killing one farm worker; five more citizens of that city were wounded. Six bombs fell on Münster wounding two people and breaking a few windows, although nothing in Münster was on the list and nobody reported bombing it.

Regardless of actual results, bombs had fallen on Germany, something which the people had been promised would never happen. The raid was a sensation, on both sides.

The British press reported a Ministry announcement made on the afternoon of 17 May:

'In support of the French Army, a squadron of Blenheims made a sortie this morning to bomb a key position at Gembloux. They encountered a large formation of enemy fighters and intense A.A. fire. In spite of great gallantry and determination 11 of our aircraft failed to return.'

The announcement didn't mention how many had set out, although the awful truth would have been apparent to those who knew what a squadron was.

The Blenheims of 82 Squadron took off at dawn from Watton, north Norfolk, to attack armoured columns including panzer units in Belgium, a few miles north-west of Namur. The promised fighter escorts did not turn up, so the formation flew alone in a clear sky, across the French coast and on towards the target. In expectation of aerial assault, the tanks were protected by batteries of light flak guns – many of them. These put up a near impenetrable curtain of fire. It was as if a dozen pheasants suddenly found themselves over a thousand twelve-bores.

The Blenheims bombed as well as they could under such a barrage. Those that emerged from the flak did so as individuals, no longer in any kind of formation, and were set upon by a flock of Me109s. As midday came, the men and women stationed at Watton aerodrome were trying to understand how it could be that only one of their aircraft had returned, and that so shot about that it never flew again.

Two days later, the squadron CO signalled 2 Group HQ that No. 82 was ready to operate again. Less than three months hence, the same squadron would attack the airfield at Aalborg. Twelve Blenheims would set out, one would turn back with technical problems and all the other eleven would be shot down.

Losses at this time of the war, although in nothing like the numbers of 1943 and '44, were doubly serious in that there was as yet no adequate system for replacing the crews that were going missing. The great majority of them were experienced regulars from before the war. New pilots were coming along – like Tiny Cooling, for example – but these were judged suitable only as second pilots. Until they had gained some experience of war, they couldn't be captains of crews.

With action being dictated by the enemy, as he advanced wherever he would, and with every daylight operation resulting in irreplaceable losses of the best men, what on earth was Bomber Command supposed to do?

There was the option of the night, but bombing armies in the dark was going to be just as dangerous and even less effective. Bombing Germany, however, seemed something of a picnic at the moment. While the *Fliegerabwehrkanonen* (flak) of the advancing German army was a very effective weapon, defence of Germany itself against air attack was not yet properly organised. Hitler and Göring had stated that no British bomb would ever fall on the Fatherland, and so flak there had been considered unnecessary, unpatriotic almost.

Hampdens, Whitleys and Wellingtons went on another record breaker, 130 aircraft, on 17/18 May, to oil refineries, railways and roads. They all came back, having lit fires in Bremen, Cologne and Hamburg, killing about fifty people and injuring another hundred and more, damaging numerous buildings and totally destroying a fertiliser factory. The oil installations were untouched but at least the airmen could see that they were having an effect.

Six Wellingtons of 9 Squadron had constituted the entire air raid on Cologne, aimed at the railway yards. Cooling was there with Douglas:

> 'We got dead on Cologne but we couldn't see our target so we bombed the alternative and started some nice fires.'

Jimmy James went to Duisburg that night, on his first op, as second pilot to Peacock in his lone Wellington, with rear gunner the ancient American Pilot Officer Bill Webster aged thirty-six.

Suddenly the moonlight was drowned by a much brighter, much more sinister light; a searing, blinding ignition that filled the eyes and painted the inside of the aircraft a brilliant white. As Peacock threw the Wimpy into a fierce diving turn, Bill Webster fired his machine guns and the white paint disappeared. Nice shooting, Bill. Yes, sure, thank you. With that little local difficulty solved, they went on to bomb what they believed to be the target and came home after six hours in the air. Jimmy James:

> 'We circled the area for at least fifteen minutes, at 10,000 feet in bright moonlight. Never a shot was fired although a searchlight turned on to us. Bill fired down the beam and it went out.'

Parachute flares illuminate a target of opportunity – roads somewhere in the Somme – while bombs explode in the middle of a field, 6 June 1940. This crew had been unable to find the main target and so had a go at something on the way home.

With its airfields threatened by the enemy's advance, the AASF began a temporary withdrawal that would soon turn permanent. Any aircraft deemed u/s were burned and abandoned. Squadrons 105 and 218 had four serviceable Battles between them; 114 and 139 had nine Blenheims. After the Blenheims were transferred, the might of the AASF consisted of six squadrons of Fairey Battles and three of Hurricanes.

While 15 Squadron was losing four out of thirteen Blenheims attacking troops at Le Cateau, 88 Squadron retreated to a new base at Les Grandes-Chappelles, a village in the Aube Département of Champagne-Ardenne, about eighty-five miles south-east of Paris. Mick Maguire:

> 'We operated mostly on dive-bombing raids and seemed to get away with it, mostly, for a while. The other squadrons which were flying low-level attacks didn't, and they had worse losses.'

The German army was keeping up the speed of its advance and making thrusts that threatened to cut off the British army, the BEF. Greatly superior fighter numbers and highly efficient anti-aircraft gunners made life extremely hazardous for the remaining Battles, and on 19 May eight went down, including three of 142 Squadron. Next day, forced into a further retreat, five more Battles, not service-able, were burned on the ground.

The situation was desperate. The French pleaded for more night bombers to attack the German advance. The RAF staff officers much preferred Germany. The compromise was ineffective.

Gordon Raphael of 77 Squadron, who had force-landed in France less than a week into the war and crashed into a French fighter, was now a Flight Lieutenant. He left Driffield in his Whitley in the evening of 18 May for an oil refinery at Hannover. He was tasked with finding the target and illuminating it with flares, which he apparently did, and on the way home was attacked by a Me110 night-fighter. He should not have been on this op at all but the award of his first medal, the DFC, had gee'd him up somewhat:

> 'I was feeling so good about getting a gong that I asked to be allowed to fly again the next night, although it wasn't my turn. On the way back, we were attacked by a Jerry over the North Sea. He shot out both my engines and busted the hydraulic system, but my rear gunner got him and he went down in flames.
>
> 'We had to land in the sea. My crew really got out in a hurry when we hit the water. I was a bit slower because I'd discovered that a bullet had gone through both my feet. We

got the dinghy out and didn't realise until later that we had it
upside down. We were picked up by a British destroyer and
I spent a couple of comfortable days in the sick bay. When I
got ashore I had to spend three months recuperating, which
was a bit annoying as it meant I missed a lot of good shows.'

The rear gunner was Aircraftman First Class Parkes who was, like
the rest, rather lucky that another bomber happened to be returning
on the same track and could call in the Royal Navy who found them
four hours later.

Group Captain Gordon Learmouth Raphael DSO, DFC and Bar,
station commander at RAF Manston, would be killed on 10 April
1945 when his Spitfire collided with a Dakota.

Northern France and Belgium offered a dozen or more targets
on the night of 20/21 May for a force of almost a hundred, the usual
mixture of Wellingtons, Hampdens and Whitleys, plus eighteen
Blenheims flying as night bombers for the first time. Two Whitleys
and a Wellington were lost over the battle area and there were
early signs of increased night-fighter defences. The bombers were
still taking off as and when, with a long time, stretching into hours,
allowed for the actual attack. Flying solo, as it were, they had no
defences but their own. One Wellington crew had an encounter with
a fighter that forced them so far off track that they couldn't get back to
bomb in the time allowed, while another had an engagement lasting
twenty minutes, with the fighter, equally new to the game, coming no
closer than 600 yards. Tiny Cooling:

'It was that peculiar time in the war when nobody was sure
about what to do. We've got this force; we'd better use it, but
how? We were showing the flag more than anything, roam-
ing the countryside in the moonlight. We didn't question
the strategy. They told us that if we saw anything worth
bombing, bomb it. I was second pilot as bomb aimer, staring
down at the patterns of hedges and fields, and if we saw a
likely looking crossroads or a railway line we'd drop a 250lb
bomb on it. It was like shooting pigeons with a blindfold on.
Kept a lot of people awake though. One night (24 May) I
listened to the King's speech on the wireless and we were off

at 22.20, over the target at midnight. We ran into accurate heavy flak and got back with a hole in the starboard wing.'

Jimmy James:

'We were bombing and machine-gunning their transport, roads and railways. It was armed reconnaissance basically, at low level. We had the Group Navigation Officer with us on this one, Sq/Ldr Graham, and he got us lost for a while. Somebody was chased by a fighter but we didn't see one. Two nights later we went with one other Wimpy from the squadron to a river bridge at Namur (River Meuse, near Charleroi, Belgium). We had a very hot reception from light flak. George (Peacock) set us up at about 2,000 feet then went into a shallow dive, the flak whizzing past us. On these low-level jobs we'd bomb at about 500 feet, when George would pull us up and we'd get a 500-foot boost when our bombs exploded. We got back with quite a lot of holes.'

The German columns were pushing for the French coast hoping to cut off the retreat of the BEF. The England-based Blenheims flew as normal, in daylight, sixty of them. They saw the roads crammed with refugees but still managed to find Germans to bomb. These raids certainly had an effect but they were much too little and far too late, and the same could be said for all of Bomber Command's efforts over the next few days – bearing in mind that Bomber Command was a relatively small force. There was a limit to what they could do, but splitting that little in half surely did not make the most of what they had, and splitting that again into many different targets meant that the ops to Germany had virtually no positive outcome.

The next night, around fifty went to all sorts of different roads and railways in The Netherlands, Belgium and France, and the following night too. The Blenheims were going by day – Calais was the target on 24 May with German troops surrounding the British garrison there. A hundred or so went to another two dozen targets on the night of 25/26 May, some into Germany and, as thirty Blenheims bombed and strafed troops during that day around the Dunkirk salient, the great water-borne evacuation began.

The Blenheims were there again next day as they would be every day until the last man left the Dunkirk beach on 3 June. The Wellingtons went most nights too, while mixed forces went to Germany and the oil.

The Luftwaffe was there less than they might have been, mainly because of the weather. The Stuka dive-bombers, as vulnerable to Spitfires and Hurricanes as Fairey Battles were to Me109s, could only operate on 27 May, the afternoon of 29 May, and 1 June. When they did attack, they were highly effective, with RAF fighters often occupied by the Stukas' protective Messerschmitts. Without the fog and the cloud on the other days, Dunkirk would surely have been much bloodier than it was.

From 21 May to 3 June, between the beginning of the retreat towards Dunkirk and the end of it, Bomber Command lost twenty-three Blenheims, six Battles, five Hampdens, four Whitleys and eight Wellingtons – as a direct result of enemy action. There were more self-inflicted wounds and some from natural causes. Three Wellingtons of 99 Squadron, for example, had to be abandoned after running out of fuel, trying to find a home landing ground in dense fog.

Compared with the two weeks before, and considering the actions they were taking and the results achieved, these losses were fairly light. Considering the size and well-being of the organisation, they were losses that were ill afforded – but, new crews were coming in.

At 102 Squadron they had the Whitley. Earlier versions of this aircraft had been barely able to reach 200mph in level flight unladen, and carrying their 7,000lb bomb load they cruised more around the 130mph mark. By this time they had Rolls-Royce Merlin engines and could make a better effort although were still very slow and cumbersome compared to the German fighters.

Relatively the opposite on the road was Leonard Cheshire's car, a Bentley Speed Six, 6.5 litre engine, top speed 84mph, one of the marque which, according to Ian Fleming, a certain Mr Bond, James Bond, had been put in store for the duration. As Cheshire disembarked among the small crowd of admiring officers around his car that afternoon was Pilot Officer Geoff Womersley (later Group Captain DSO, DFC) who, as well as flying regular ops, was responsible for getting the squadron's new boys' flying up to scratch.

Later in the war, pilots would arrive on squadron with 450 hours in their log books flying single, twin and four-engined aircraft, plus another fifty or so on the Link flight simulation trainer. RAF Bomber

Aircraft Type and No.	Crew.	Duty.	Time Up.	Time Down.	Details of Sortie or Flight.	References.
Wellington L. 7799.	P/O. WALSH. SGT. CANTON. SGT. BRUCE. SGT. COSTAIN. P/O. VAUGHAN. SGT. COOPER.		2350	0320	In accordance with H.Q. No. 3 Group form B. 151 dated 26th May, 1940, four aircraft carried out raids against JUMET aerodrome. Three aircraft found and bombed the target, the fourth aircraft was unable, due to darkness, to locate the target. At the time of take-off the weather between	
P. 9239.	SGT. BULL. SGT. BROOKS. SGT. BETTS. SGT. GANNON. SGT. PETERS. SGT. DOBSON.		2340	0250	HONINGTON and the ENGLISH COAST was good, visibility being about 6 miles. From the ENGLISH COAST to the target, slightly hazy, average visibility, 5/10ths. high clouds at 10,000'. These conditions remained throughout the period.	
N. 2942.	F/O. TURNER. P/O. BERRY. SGT. ROGERS. SGT. POWIS. SGT. WHITTLE. SGT. GIBB.		0005	0345	Two aircraft carried out high level bombing, one at 10,000 feet, one at 7,000'. The third aircraft carried out a gliding approach attack from 10,000' to 5,000'. This type of attack proved very successful as very little opposition was met from A.A. guns. The bombs were dropped in sticks, two to three runs being made by each aircraft.	
N. 2898.	F/LT. FORDHAM. P/O. NICHOLSON. SGT. ORCHARD. SGT. NICHOLLS. P/O. MARSHALL. SGT. PATTERSON.		2340	0435	Two aircraft made full use of delayed action parachute flares and these again proved highly successful in that not only did they light up the target area, but attracted a considerable amount of A.A. fire.	

Anatomy of an air raid. Four Wellingtons went to an aerodrome at night. One couldn't find it 'due to darkness.' The other three tried to hit it in three different ways. Such descriptions of an air raid make it sound like a leisurely gentleman's pursuit. Two or three runs, gliding in, very little opposition equating to success; what changes would be wrought in the life and death of a bomber in the years to come. Whether to bomb this way or that was a decision made by the captains at the target, if they got there. When skippers did find what they believed to be it, some favoured a low-level run, some a diving run, some a gliding run with the engines throttled back so the enemy would not be so aware of their approach, some an orthodox high-level run. What was considered high at that time would be considered low later.

Command in 1940 was not quite so fussy, especially if the chaps were the right sort. Womersley:

> 'Cheshire arrived with about fifty hours on Tiger Moths. I was the squadron instructor and he was among the first pilots sent to us from the university air squadron. He'd had no twin-engined training at all, so I took him up in a Whitley for day and night flying.'

It wasn't quite as bad as Womersley remembered. Cheshire, who would become Group Captain Baron Cheshire, VC, OM, DSO and Two bars, DFC and one of the most celebrated flyers of the bomber war, had had seven months basic training, plus two months on twin-engined aircraft at No. 10 OTU, including fourteen hours' night flying on instruments. According to his story, *Bomber Pilot*, until his first op he hadn't seen a navigator before:

> 'I never knew there could be so much stuff for what I imagined was a simple operation. Maps, rulers, compass, dividers, CSC, pencils, rubber, penknife, code books, plotter, astro tables, watch, sextant, planisphere, protractor, log book and Very cartridges.'

The CSC (Course/Speed Computer) was a little mechanical device which calculated course differences according to variations observed in wind speed and direction. Like all such devices, it depended entirely on the accuracy of the input data. The planisphere was a map of the stars.

The feeling of 'I never knew' continued right through Cheshire's first op. The business of flying a route in the dark, finding the target, bombing it and coming home, was so complex that it can hardly seem credible to modern folk used to getting in a car and going from A to B with one finger on the steering wheel and one ear tuned to the satnav.

'I think we're there. Better drop a flare. Wireless op?'

'Yes, sir, flare ready.'

'Let her go. Rear gunner, can you see anything? Has the flare gone yet?'

'No, not yet, captain. Yes, there it is, burning OK. Can't see the town though.'

'All right. I'll turn on to it and have a look.'

Cheshire was listening to this on his intercom, utterly confused by flares, fires and flak and unable to tell one from the other:

> 'Lofty (pilot) was circling steeply. I wondered how he could do it without watching his instruments, and felt frightened lest he should spin in. We dropped two more flares. The others seemed to know what they were doing, but I had lost all sense of direction.'

Later in the war, a much more highly trained pilot would be put in charge of a four-engined bomber and six men and be expected to take the lot to Germany and back, without any experience of knowing what he was doing. For now, new pilots had to serve their apprenticeship.

ORB, 9 Squadron:

> 'In accordance with HQ No. 3 Group operation order form B 156, dated 31st May 1940, 12 aircraft of this squadron carried out raids against the road junctions at SOEX. Nine aircraft found and bombed the correct target, two aircraft bombed the roadway in the village of WARMHOUDT which was 5 miles away from the target. One aircraft was unable to locate the primary target and therefore bombed the secondary target, which was NIEUPORT.'

Cooling found it all right:

> 'Took off 21.40, back 00.30, bed 01.30. Bombed Soest, south of Dunkirk. Place all in flames. Terrible sight.'

When the evacuation from Dunkirk was almost complete, attention switched back to Germany with another 100+ raid, but a few Wellingtons headed for German positions in France in a last desperate attempt to buy the retreating soldiers some time. Tiny Cooling, 3 June:

> 'As we crossed the Suffolk coast near Southwold we could see two sunsets. One was the fires at Dunkirk. There were several other Wellingtons near us and it was one of the times

I really felt I was doing something. Dougie had put me as first pilot on this sortie and I joined in a small formation with some other aircraft. Each was flying along, rising up and down on its own individual air currents, and I felt quite a surge of emotion. I'd recently seen the Laurence Olivier film of Henry V and it seemed just right, the band of brothers, and gentlemen in England now a-bed shall think themselves accursed they were not here.

'The Wimpys went their separate ways and when we got to Dunkirk we made our approach high and to the south, avoiding the Royal Navy whose aircraft recognition wasn't so hot at that time. The sea was like a new sheet of beaten copper, with movement frozen by our height and the thousands of waves reflecting the glow of the blaze all about. We had sixteen two-fifty bombs which we dropped one at a time, hoping that we'd keep a few German heads down so that another boatload of our boys could get away.'

With Dunkirk over but France still fighting, the same split in priorities still applied. Unlike the ferociously efficient anti-aircraft defences of the Wehrmacht and their swarms of supporting fighters, the fatherland's urban equivalent, believed until recently by the Germans to be more or less unnecessary, was inadequate and scrambling about for a co-ordinated system which would work. Cooling:

'As a force we were grotesquely under trained, but so were the Germans. They didn't know what to do about it either and on one trip to Germany seemingly they were trying something fresh. Flying searchlights. We were picked up by a light so we flew up into some cloud, and above it, and so did the searchlight. We couldn't get the cloud between us and the light. We heard later that several crews reported Me110s carrying searchlights, which seemed a ridiculous idea, and we never heard of it or saw it again but we came back convinced we had been lit up by a flying searchlight. It was a highly disconcerting experience.'

On the night of 5/6 June, ninety bombers were divided between railway targets in Germany and battle targets in the Somme. Hamburg reported ten fires. Duisburg, which was where Peacock, James and Webster were going, made no such report.

A city target by night must have seemed almost a relief after all that diving into German army flak. Civil defences were still not up to the job, nor the night-fighters. Once they were through the Wehrmacht gun positions at the Dutch coast they could feel themselves free-ish agents of the darkness.

The squadron CO, Square McKee, always went to the control tower to say a last word to the boys flying on operations. He would wait until the bomber had taken off and then speak on the radio telephone. His message was always economical and always the same. 'Good luck.' Pilots, especially the superstitious ones, which was almost all of them, generally had a stock reply. Peacock always said 'So long, sir'. Tonight, he said something different. He said 'Goodbye'. McKee was taken aback. 'Come off it, George,' he said. 'We never say goodbye.' There was no response from Peacock.

An hour later, they were across the sea and approaching enemy territory. As they reached it, where the rivers Rhine and Maas join, south-west of Rotterdam, searchlights probed the sky and this time there was no putting them out. They were caught, and held long enough for a heavy flak shell to find them. No one was wounded but the port engine was on fire and the flames were growing and licking back. Soon theirs would be an aircraft with only one wing. Bill Webster:

> 'The pilot gave the order to put on parachutes. I called him
> up on the intercom but as I got no reply I baled out.'

It wasn't quite as simple as that, was it, Bill? For a start, parachute training in Bomber Command consisted of being shown how to put the pack on and which was the doo-dah you pulled to open it. 'Well, there's a first time for everything', Webster might have thought as he swung his rear turret open. Those turrets swung around to starboard. His way out therefore was on the port side, where all the flames were.

Hesitating, hanging half out of the turret, uncertain if his parachute would catch fire, Bill got his leg caught in his guns. Uncertainties became academic as the flames spread and the aircraft went into a steep dive with Webster trapped. As the dive increased in speed and angle, his chest-mounted parachute pack whipped up past his head

SECRET.
M.I.9/S/P.G./LIB./32.
IN GERMAN HANDS.   LIBERATED
BY ALLIED FORCES.

The information contained in this report is to be treated as

SECRET.
STATEMENT BY

77955 F/Lt. Sedgwick Whitcley WEBSTER, 9 Sqn., Bomber Command, R.A.F.

Captured: Nr. ROTTERDAM 6 Jun 40.   Liberated: LUBECK 2 May 45.
Left   : BRUSSELS 7 May 45.   Arrived : U.K. 7 May 45.

Date of Birth   : 28 Oct 04.   Peacetime Profession: Advertising.
Date of Enlistment: Mar 40.   Private Address; Barclays Bank,
Post in Crew   : Rear Gunner.   6, Mount Street,
                                                       LONDON, W.1.

OTHER MEMBERS OF CREW:

        S/Ldr. PEACOCK   (pilot)(killed)
        P/O JAMES   (2nd pilot)(P/W)
        Sgt. HARGREAVES   (navigator)(P/W)
        Sgt. GRIFFITHS   (wireless operator)(P/W)
        Sgt. MURTON   (mid upper gunner)(P/W)

1. CAPTURE.

        We took off from HONINGTON in a Wellington aircraft at 2140 hours
on 5 Jun 40 on a bombing mission. On the way to the target the aircraft
was hit by Flak and set on fire. The pilot gave the order to put on parachutes. I called up the pilot on the inter-comm, but as I got no reply,
I baled out.

        I landed in a field about 15 km. South of ROTTERDAM at 2330 hrs. I
hid my parachute, harness and map west and then walked to a house and asked
for help. This was refused and I made my way to a railway track intending
to follow it. After a short time I decided that it would be best to get to
a road as I was unaware of my exact location. I walked across country to
a road and I was captured by a German patrol about an hour after baling out.

        On 6 Jun I was taken by car to ROTTERDAM and then to AMSTERDAM, where
I was interrogated briefly. Later that day I met Sgts. GRIFFITHS and MURTON
of my crew. In the afternoon we were taken by car to DULAG LUFT (OBERURSEL).

                            /2. CAMPS IN WHICH IMPRISONED.

INTERVIEWED BY: I.S.9(W) 24 May 45.

Distribution of this Report: APPENDIX C.
D.D.M.I.(P/W).   Distribution:
I.S.9.   D.D.M.I.(P/W).
I.S.9(W).   I.S.9.
A.I.1(a)P/W (2 copies).   I.S.9(X).
H.Q., Bomber Command, R.A.F.   I.S.9(W)(File).
A.L.O., M.I.9.
File.

```
2.  CAMPS IN WHICH IMPRISONED.

          DULAG LUFT (OBERURSEL)          7 - 10 Jun 40.
          STALAG XII A (LIMBURG)          10 - 14 Jun 40.
          OFLAG II A (PRENSLAU)           14 Jun - 4 Jul 40.
          STALAG LUFT I (BARTH)           5 Jul 40 - Apr 42.
          STALAG LUFT III (SAGAN)         Apr 42 - 28 Jan 45.
          MARLAG-MILAG NORD (WESTERTIMKE) 6 Feb - 10 Apr 45.

3.  ATTEMPTED ESCAPE.

        From Apr 42 until Apr 43 I was engaged in the construction of three
tunnels in the East compound, STALAG LUFT III (SAGAN).  None of these tunnels
was successful.

4.  LIBERATION.

        On 2 May 45 I was liberated by Allied forces near LUBECK.  I was sent
to LUNEBURG and BRUSSELS, from where I was sent by air to the U.K. on 7 May.
```

In Bill Webster's post-liberation interview, he does not seem to know that his fellow crewman Sergeant Ronnie Hargrave, here as Hargeaves, was killed.

in the wind. The chute opened with a crack and the sudden force of it hauled Webster clear, leaving only a little skin, blood and RAF cloth behind when he might have left a whole limb. Jimmy James:

'Four flak batteries opened up on us and the port engine caught fire. The skipper gave the order to bale out. Hargrave, Griffiths and I left by the front hatch but Ronnie Hargrave's parachute caught fire and he fell all the way and was killed. Murton left from the centre, Webster from the rear turret. We saw our aircraft blow up and go in. The skipper had no chance to get out himself.'

It was a matter of unbreakable honour that the captain held his machine steady while the others jumped. One had jumped in vain. His parachute was touched by the fire and that was that, a brief candle falling to earth with no possibility of survival.

The white-painted village church of Simonshaven has only a small graveyard. In the south-eastern corner of it were placed the bodies of Squadron Leader George Ernest Peacock DFC, aged twenty-six, of the Durham town of Spennymoor, and Sergeant Ronald Charles Hargrave DFM, aged twenty-five, of the Warwickshire borough of Sutton Coldfield.

Webster, Jimmy James and Sergeants Murton and Griffiths survived. The nice, friendly fellow who was very probably the first American bomber aircrew in the RAF, thus became the first American to be shot down with Bomber Command. Soon he became the first American airman taken prisoner in Europe:

> 'I landed in a field about 15km south of Rotterdam. I hid my parachute, harness and Mae West, then walked to a house and asked for help. This was refused and I made my way to a railway track intending to follow it. Unaware of my exact location I walked across country to a road and I was captured by a German patrol about an hour after baling out.'

After interrogation in Amsterdam, Webster was displayed in Berlin with the other officer, Jimmy James. The locals, who had seen countless foreigners before the war, now found them as curious as Martians. On they went via three short-term imprisonments to Stalag Luft I, their home, they must have expected, for the duration. Jimmy James:

> 'It was about a year after our capture and we were in Stalag Luft I, Barth, and Bill Webster was in the top bunk above me. One night, everybody in the hut was woken by a noise, and somebody got up and put the light on. There was Bill, lying on the floor groaning but not too badly hurt, and he said "I was dreaming. I thought I'd bailed out of a Wimpy".'

They would both end up in Stalag Luft III where, in 1942/43, Webster worked on three tunnel digs in the East compound, none of them successful, and James would take part in – and survive – the Great Escape of March 1944. By the time Bill was liberated in 1945, he was a flight lieutenant with a lot of back-pay due.

CHAPTER 8

One War Ends and Another Begins

While the RAF had been struggling for air supremacy over Dunkirk, the German armour switched its main objective to Paris. The AASF was still in France, reducing in numbers by the day and falling back again and again to new airfields.

From Les Grand Chappelles aerodrome, Maguire's 88 Squadron retreated to a large space mown out of the middle of a wheatfield, 250 miles to the west of Mourmelon by the village of Moizy, near the river Loire. Maguire:

'That was one good thing about the Battle. It could take off and land anywhere. Our sister squadron, 218, had been more or less wiped out and one or two of our aircrew got very nervous, not surprisingly. (No. 218 Squadron had lost four aircraft on the second day of the blitzkrieg and five at Sedan.) One night we were doing the pre-take-off test where they opened and closed the bombs doors, and when this particular pilot did it a forty pounder fell out onto the ground. He did it again and the same thing happened. I got up on the wing and looked into the bomb bay while he did it yet again and I saw a spark. This pilot had a tin hat over his flying helmet and he was sitting on another. He'd got himself in such a state that he'd switched the bomb release to number one position, which dropped the bombs. We got him sorted out and as he taxied to his take-off position he

165

crashed into the Chance light and spread his aircraft all over the field.'

The Chance light was a floodlight mounted on top of a three-ton truck, so called because the manufacturers of the glass were Messrs Chance, and it shone brightly and for long enough for each aircraft to take off and land.

Maguire:

'On another night I'd taken the pins out of an aircraft's bombs, which made them live, and as usual given the pins to the observer so he could put them back in if they were forced to land with the bombs still aboard. I had three aircraft to look after and this was the front one, with a pilot called Clark. The engine was started – they were an early version of the Merlin engine – and a stick of German bombs burst right in front of us. I dived under the tailplane where I was joined by another pilot, McLaughlin (later to lose an arm defending Malta), and the third one who kept asking where his service revolver was. I could feel it under my hand, so I passed it to him and told him to shut up about his effing revolver. Clark cut the engine and jumped out, and then we noticed the wireless op lying on the ground. He'd been leaning against one of the wheels.

'McLaughlin got the morphine and we put the man on the back of a truck and off he went. The airfield was u/s and one of our aircraft, which had been taking off when the bombs fell, had gone straight into a crater. The others began to walk back while I put the pins back in the bombs, when I noticed the tip of the propellor. It was normally yellow but in the dawn light I could see it had blood on it, and scattered around I could see pieces of Bakelite from a set of earphones. McLaughlin came up, said there was an arm over there, and was sick on my feet. I got a map out of the cockpit, wrapped the arm in it, put it back on the ground, and headed back to the Ops room, which was a shed. The CO was in there. "What's it like out at dispersals?" he said. I said "There's an arm up there, wrapped in a map." "The chap's dead," said the CO, "we'll bury him this afternoon." "He'd better have his arm back, then," I said, and set off to find it. McLaughlin was sure I'd be court martialed for insubordination.'

What was left of the AASF withdrew to the region round Orleans and Le Mans. From here they attacked troop movements and communications. There would be more withdrawals before they escaped from the west coast. During this final period the Battles operated mainly by night, and with few losses. To quote the *R.A.F. Short Official History*:

> 'Flying and landing a Battle by night was no easy task – there was a brilliant glare from the exhaust which dazzled the pilot, and the view from the observer's seat was poor – but those difficulties which were not overcome were ignored, and there was an immediate and dramatic decline in the casualty rate. During the intense daylight operations of May 10–14, one aircraft had been lost in every two sorties; during the night operations of May 20–June 4 the loss was just over one in every two hundred ... (Night bombing) however was by no means all gain, for safety could only be achieved at the expense of accuracy. In fact so many Battle crews now dropped their bombs with no more precise identifications of their target than that provided by their watches, that Barratt was compelled to forbid bombing on "estimated time of arrival". After that the phrase ceased to appear in the pilots' reports. The practice, however, continued.'

The Germans were advancing inexorably while a few Bomber and Fighter Command squadrons tried to slow their progress and the mighty Luftwaffe destroyed more or less everybody who interfered. When on 11 June the Germans broke through the French positions on the Marne, Oise, and Seine, the last line of resistance, there was no hope left for the AASF. If they stayed, they would be utterly destroyed. Barratt ordered them back to England.

Mick Maguire prepared his aircraft for their last France-based operation on 13 June, bombing the German army in the Forêt de Gault, Marne. As was customary, if there was any chance of an hour's kip, it was taken under the aircraft tail if the sun was shining hot:

'I was woken up by someone shooting a rifle. He was firing at a man running away, heading for the growing corn. One of the armourers was still up on the aircraft seeing to the machine gun. He just turned it on the man and fired. We buried him that day but we never found out who he was. There were plenty of stories about, of sabotage and fifth columnists and so on. The engine fitter who'd been firing the rifle had been asleep too, and woken to find this man trying to slash the tyres of the aircraft. I said you should have let him. He'd have died a bit sooner because it would have blown him to pieces.'

Only one Battle failed to return from that final trip, downed by Me109s with the crew surviving, and on 14 June the flying part of No. 88 went back to England. In the chaos of France's defeat, transport had not been laid on for the armourers. They liberated a Dodge truck from the French and headed west, following the Loire for some 150 miles and ending up at Nantes.

Elements of 73 Squadron and most of No. 98 were with the thousands of men, women and children aboard HMT *Lancastria* in the Loire estuary off St-Nazaire. Of the 4,000 or more killed when the Germans bombed the ship, ninety were from 98 Squadron. The armourers from 88 were supposed to be with them but they were too late. Mick Maguire:

'It was midnight, black dark, our aircraft had gone and we had to try to get back to Blighty somehow. We piled into a brand new Dodge truck which had somehow been acquired from the French and which we modified by taking off the covers and fitting a couple of Lewis guns to fire forward and aft. We went to Nantes, which was silently seething with troops and air force, including a regiment of Canadian soldiers in kilts who had landed to fight the Germans and been ordered back onto their ship again. It was chaos. Apparently we had been supposed to embark on the *Lancastria*, which we later found out had taken a bomb right down her funnel and sunk with everyone lost, a story which was suppressed at the time.

'Our practice had been to give our rations away to the passing refugees. My pal McGivern was good at that. He used to give my rations away as well as his own. He did us a better turn in Brest because he found a truck that had overturned which was full of strawberries, so we went with every container we could lay our hands on and picked strawberries while the Luftwaffe was trying to mine the harbour to stop us getting out. We had a ship by then, a tramp steamer, but we couldn't go because of the mines so we searched for more provisions and found a NAAFI van which was well stocked with Black and White whisky. After filling our water bottles with that we came across a supply of fresh bread, so we had our picnic ready.'

Some interfering officer spotted their new Dodge and ordered them and it down to the harbour, to machine gun it, run it into the water and to dump all their kit after it except for one blanket each:

'McGivern still had his guitar and I had my tandem bicycle. I don't know what happened to the guitar but I knocked on the door of a small café and, eventually, when the woman had slid back all the bolts and turned all the locks, I said "Madamoiselle, pour vous, une bicyclette," at which she burst into tears. I suppose she'd expected me to be German.'

Back at their picnic spot, thoroughly ready for some refreshment, they were settling into their bread, strawberries and whisky when two Bren carriers turned up and parked next to the airmen:

'These soldiers in black overalls climbed out and we asked them where the rearguard was, because we were in Brest and there was nowhere further to go. They said they were the rearguard. So we invited them for tea and they joined us after they'd run their Bren carriers into the sea.
'When we did board our ship the captain said "Nobody go below. Take your boots off and hang them round your neck." He thought we might hit a mine. I edged my way to the rail at the side, ready to dive over, and I found I'd been followed. It was someone I'd been in training with and I asked him why

he was following me. He said "I was with you at Eastchurch. I remember you. You were in the swimming team." '

On an English quayside at last, Maguire and his mates were astonished to see uniformed Customs officers approaching:

'They were looking for dogs. The RAF seemed to attract stray dogs and French strays were not wanted in the UK. We had two little dogs with us so we all lined up, stood to attention, hid the dogs in among us and sang 'Abide with Me' at the tops of our voices so the Customs boys wouldn't hear the barking.'

Coastal radar picked up a distress signal from Wellington WS/P-Peter coming back from Germany, tracked it, and lost it on 19 June. The signal had been too weak to do much more than identify the aircraft but at 05.30 Square McKee was up with the standby crew, heading out to sea to search for Frank Butler. After only a couple of hours' sleep, Jock Gilmour woke Tiny Cooling to tell him he was a captain today. They would take off at 09.30 and go and help find Butler. Cooling:

'We began our sweeps 50 miles out, halfway to Holland. While the gunners searched the sea for a little yellow dot of a dinghy, and the sky for a little black dot of a fighter, I flew at 600 feet in ever increasing rectangles, making 90 degree turns and lengthening the line each time until we'd drawn a straight-sided Catherine wheel and were 20 miles off the enemy coast. Then I flew to another starting point and did it over again.

'If we found them, we'd have to circle over them with the telegraph key pressed down, so the rescue people could get a good bearing. This would alert the Germans too and we could expect interference from them by sea and air. But, we didn't find anything. We got excited about a yellow oil drum, but that's all it was. Nobody found anything. They were down there on the sea bottom, Butler and his men.'

There were few confirmed ditchings but many aircraft which failed to return from Germany for unknown reasons were searched for if some sort of fix had indicated a possible sea crash and, until naviga-tion improved greatly, there would be plenty of those. Sometimes a whole squadron, back from an op in the early hours, would take to the air again to scour the ocean for a lost comrade, sometimes close to the enemy coast. While this may have done wonders for squadron

Tom Kirby-Green, seen here with his wife, flew with 9 Squadron in early 1940 and was shot down, as Squadron Leader with 40 Squadron, the only survivor of his Wellington and that only just. He recovered from his spinal injuries to take a leading part in tunnelling at Stalag Luft III.

morale and team spirit, it clearly became less and less of a good idea as German fighters increased in numbers and skill. The practice was eventually stopped.

The Germans reached Paris on 16 June. ORB, 9 Squadron, 22 June:

> 'France signed armistice. Weather fair becoming cloudy with light rain after dark. Nothing of operational importance occurred.'

With remarkable ease the Germans had taken as much of mainland Europe as they seemed to want for the moment: neighbours Poland, Denmark, Norway, Holland, Belgium, Luxembourg and France. Britain surely had to be next and the only way to hit the Germans back was by air. For attacking, for prosecuting the war, RAF Bomber Command was it. There wasn't anything else.

Promoted while in prison, Flight Lieutenant Michael Casey was shot down in a Blenheim of 57 Squadron, 16 October 1939. Other names featured in this book are Les Bull and Tom Kirby-Green of 9 Squadron.

Bibliography

Bomber Command Losses of the Second World War. W. R. Chorley
Bomber Pilot. Leonard Cheshire
Bombers Battle. A Wing Commander
Enemy Coast Ahead. Guy Gibson
It's Suicide But It's Fun. Chris Goss
The Battle of Heligoland Bight. Robin Holmes
The Bomber Command War Diaries. Martin Middlebrook and Chris
  Everitt
The Fight at Odds. Denis Richards
The Last Flight of AD730. Colin Hill
The Luftwaffe War Diaries. Cajus Bekker
Wellington at War. Chaz Bowyer

Many and various websites including acesofww2.com/Canada,
aircrewwremembrancesociety.com, ww2today.com